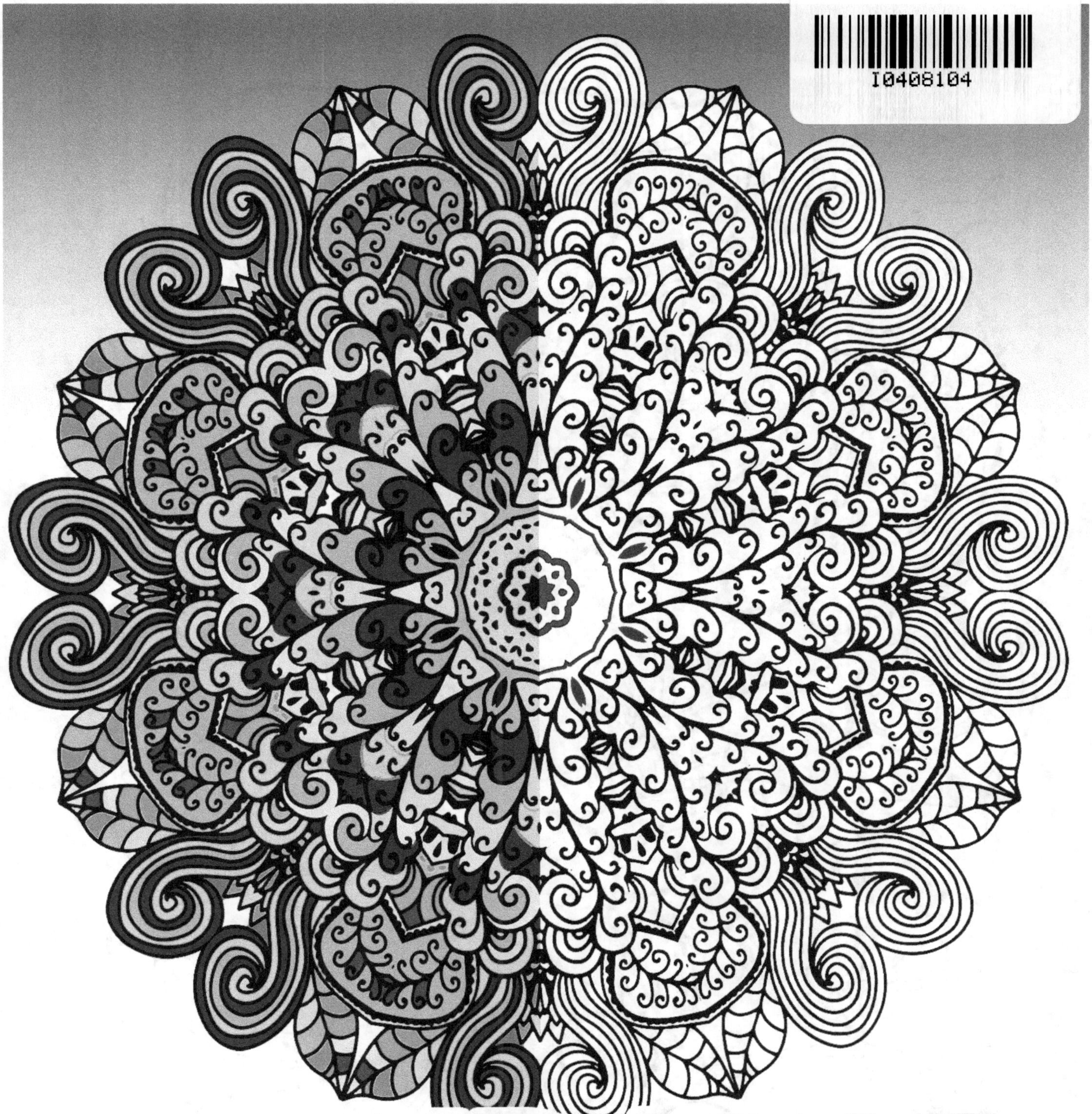

MANDALAS

COLORING BOOK FOR ADULTS

Art Therapy Designs

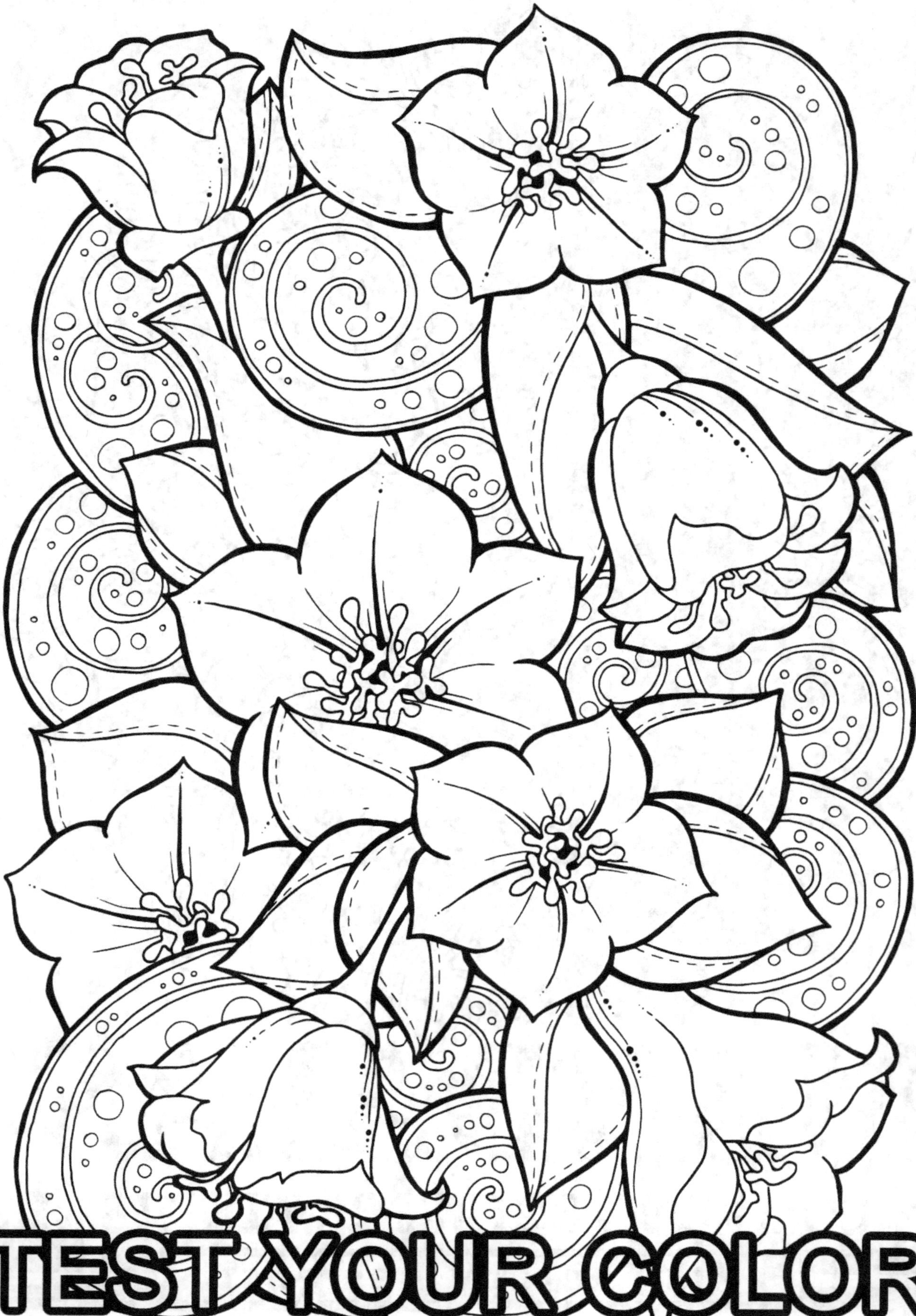

TEST YOUR COLOR

TEST YOUR COLOR

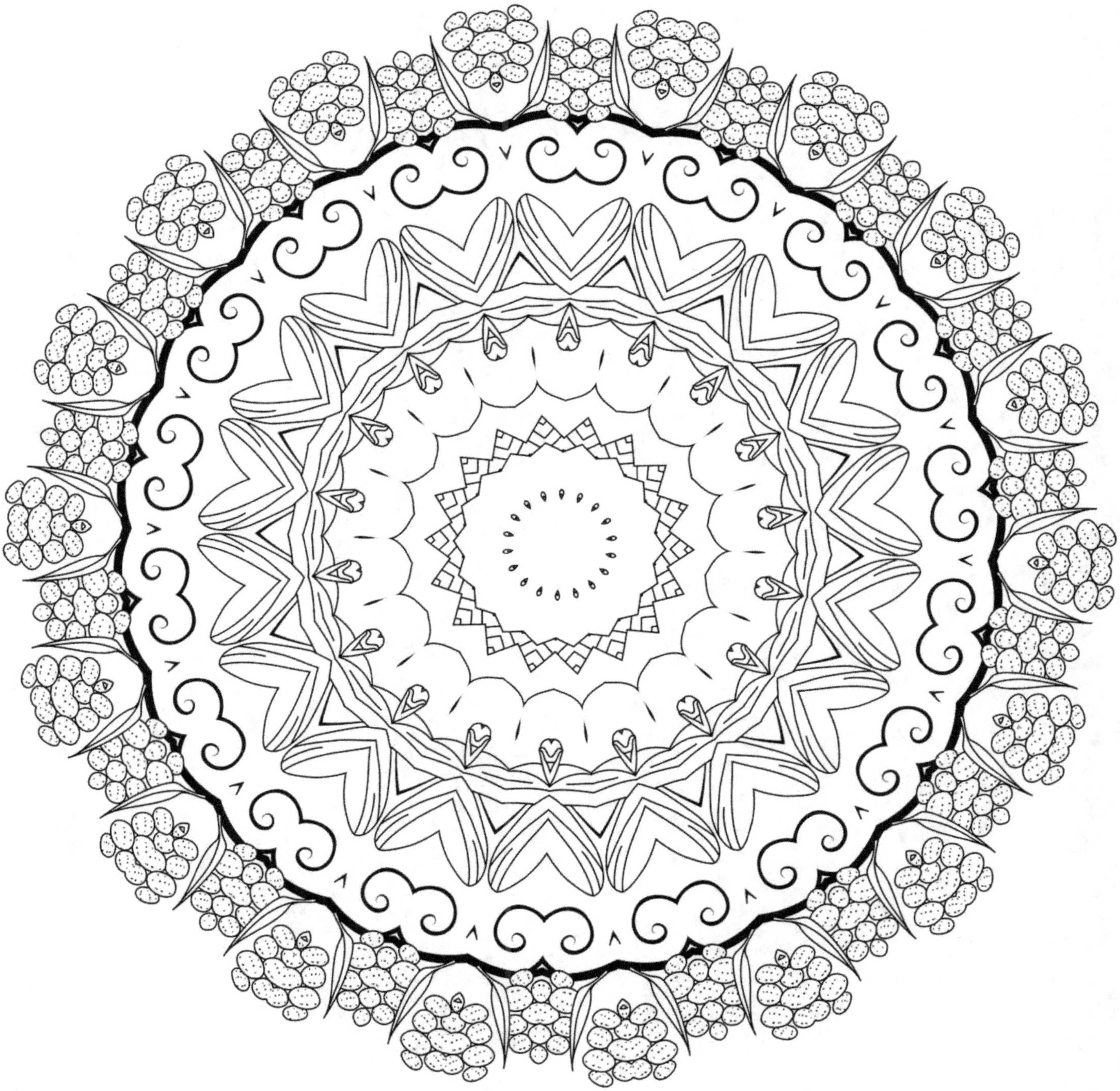

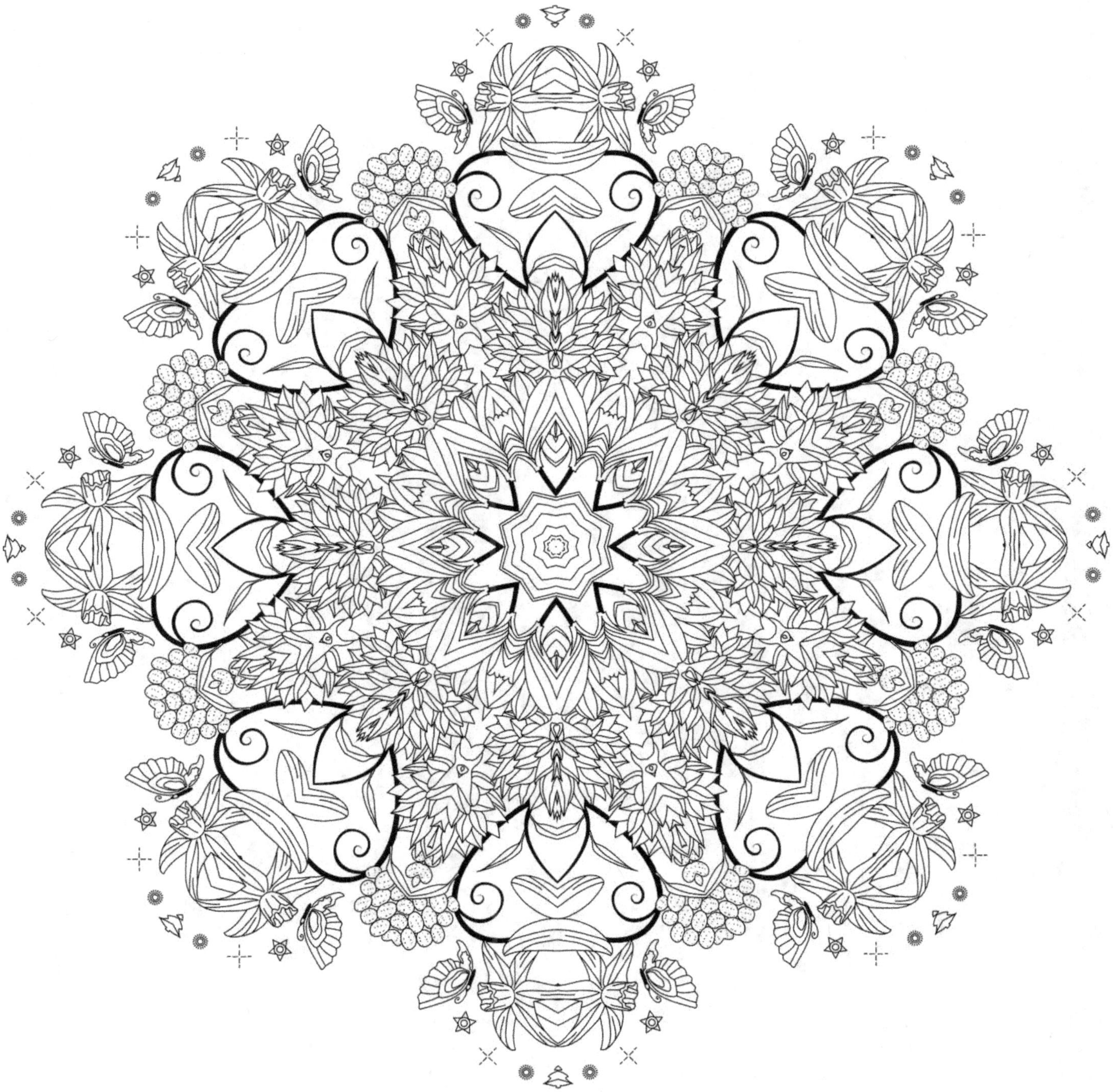

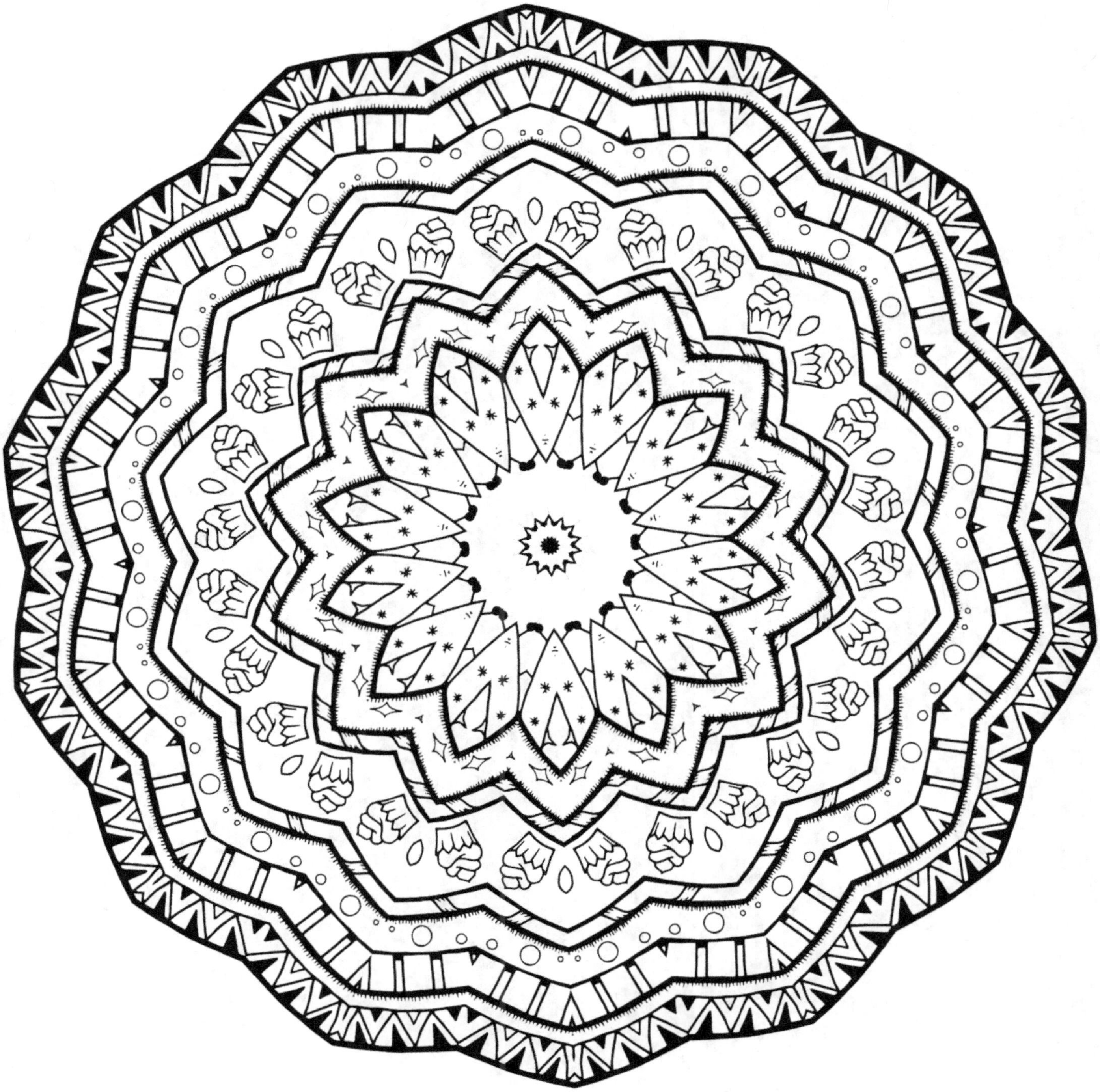

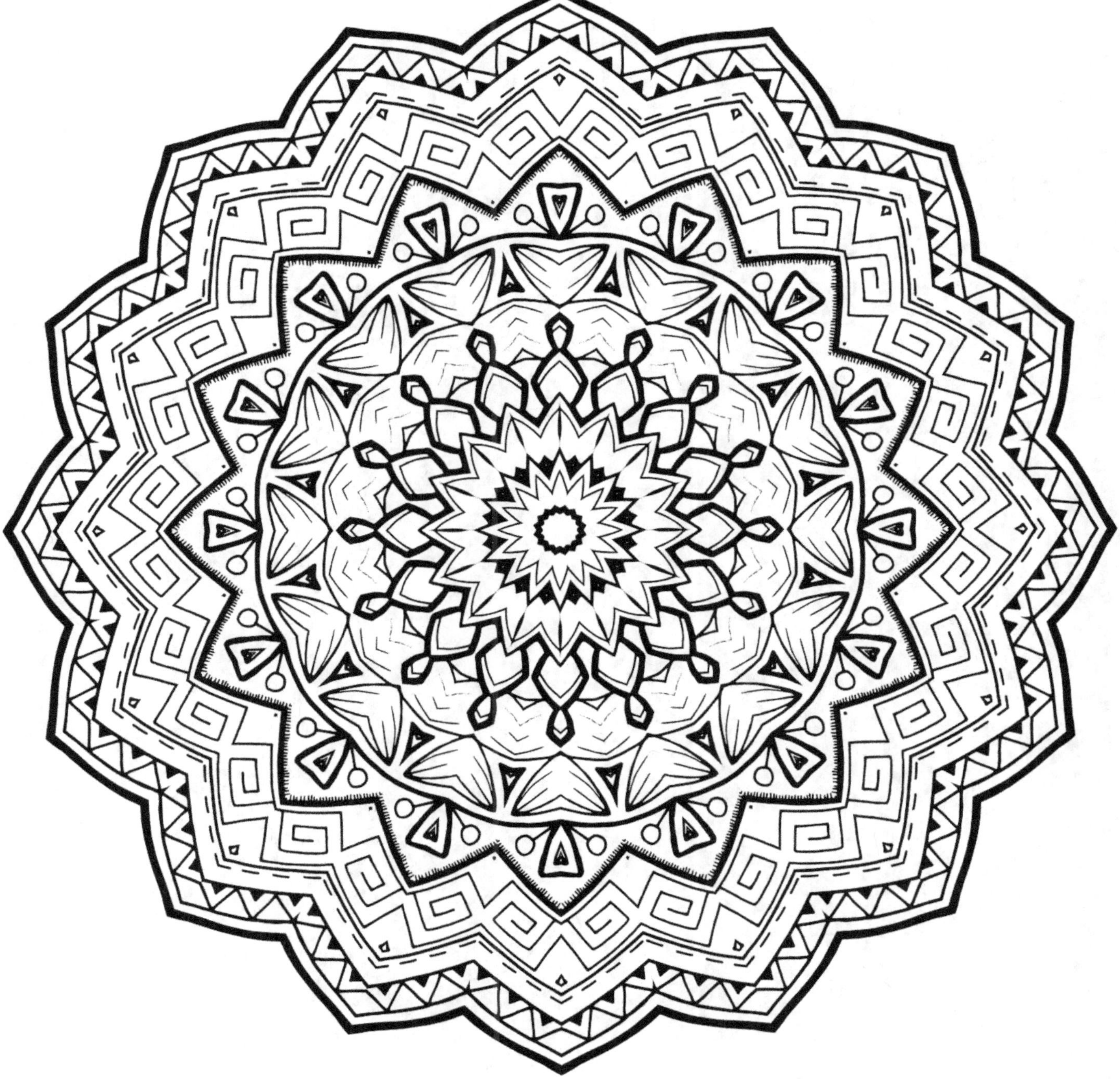

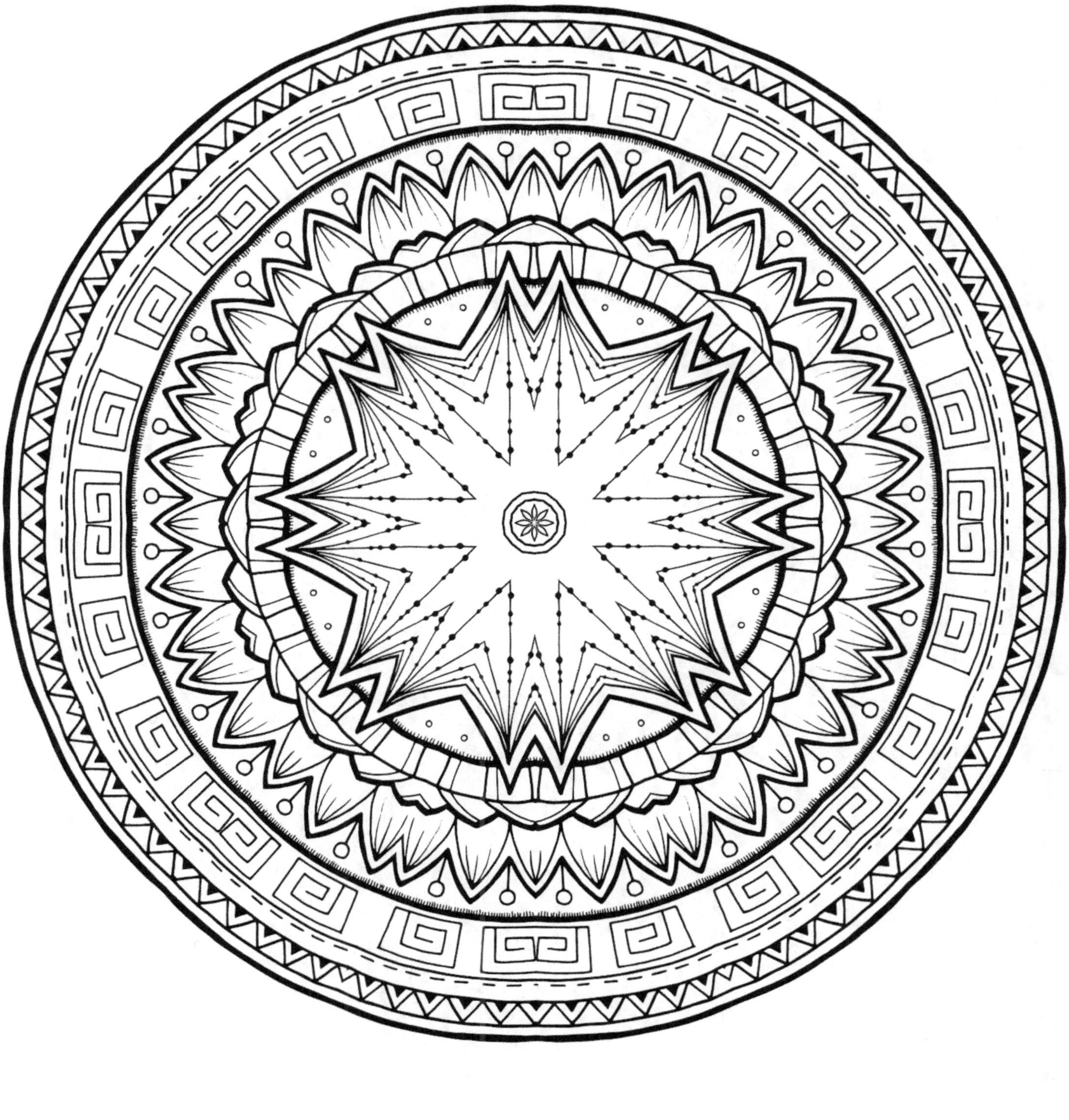

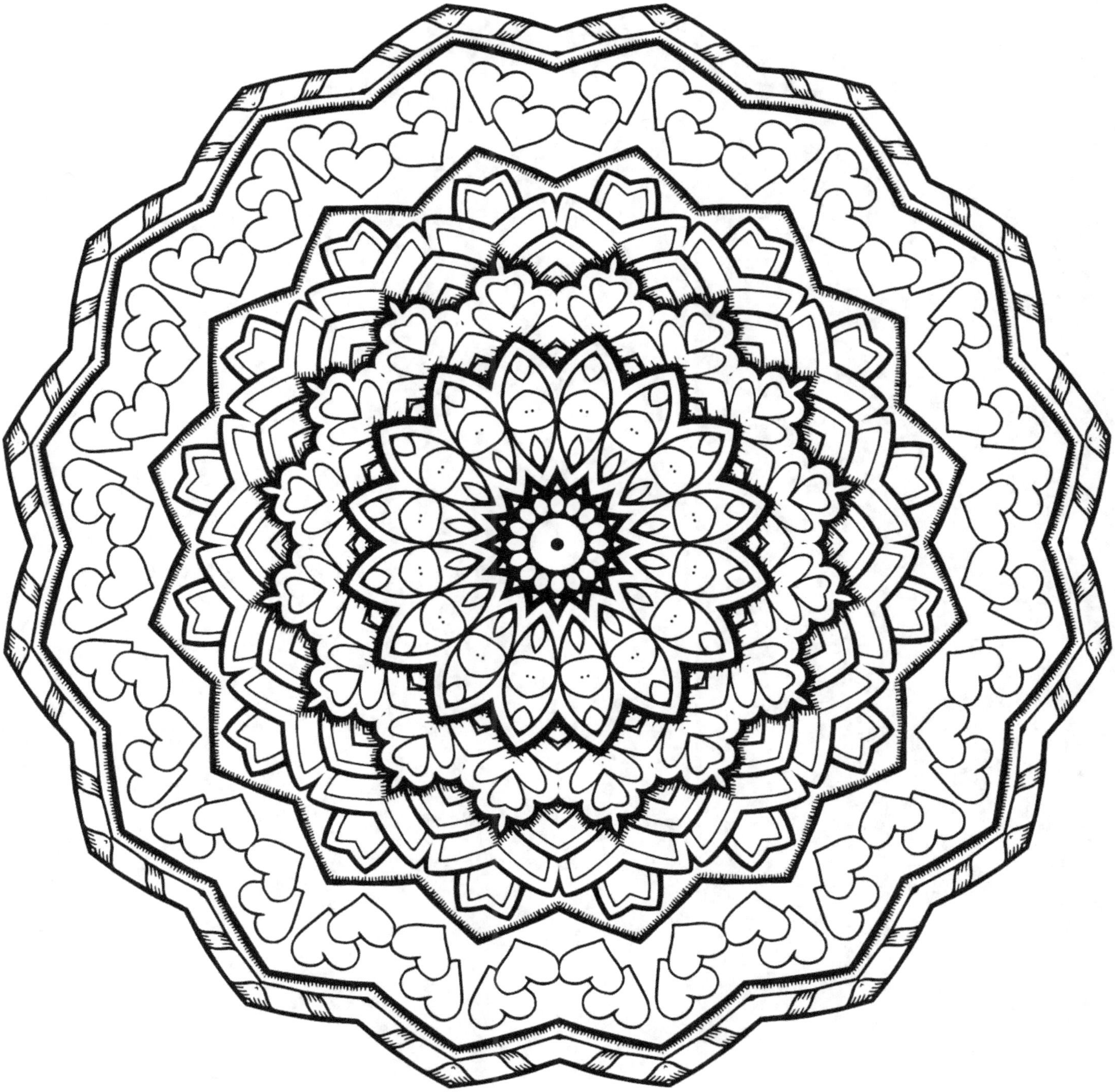

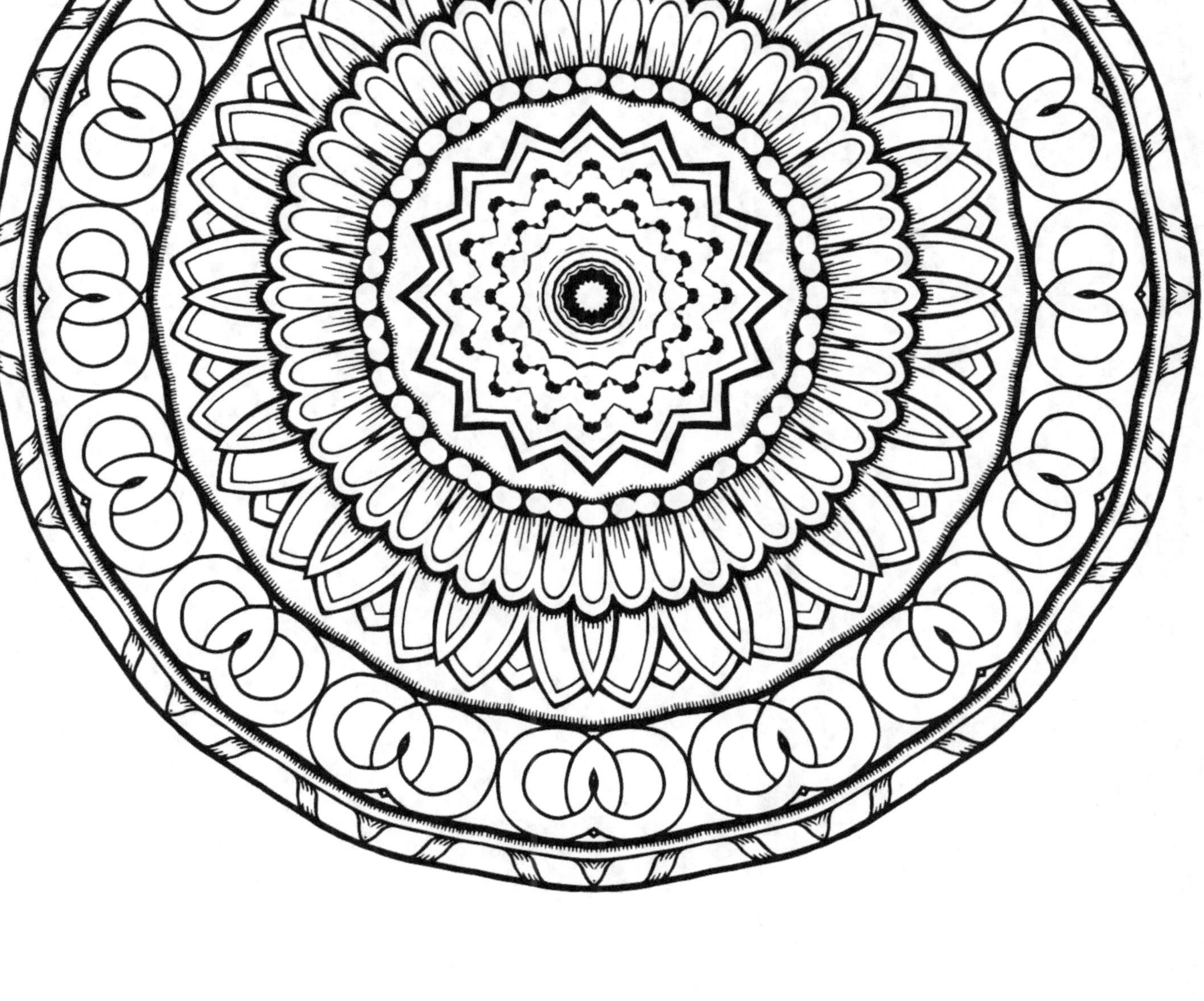

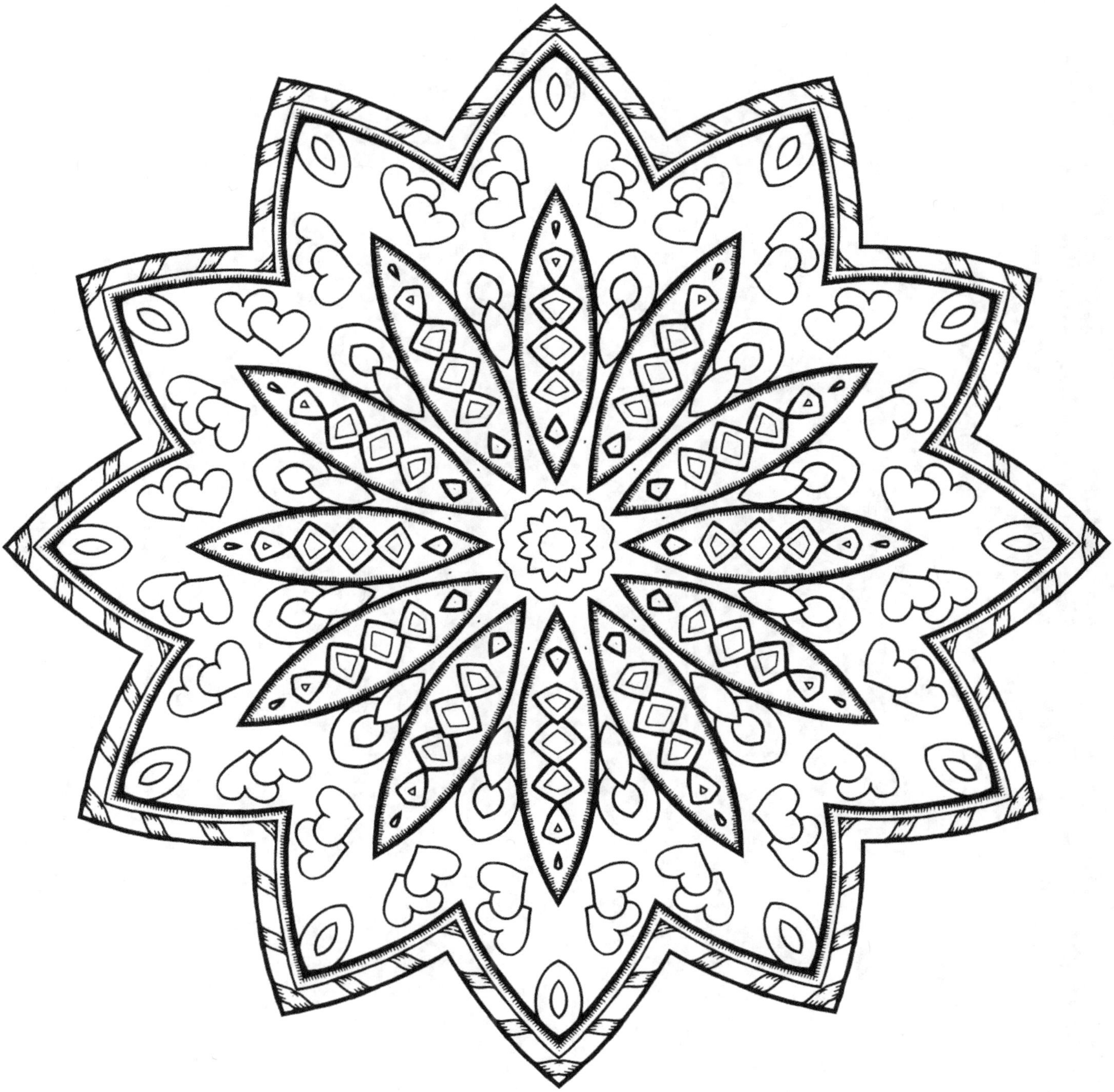

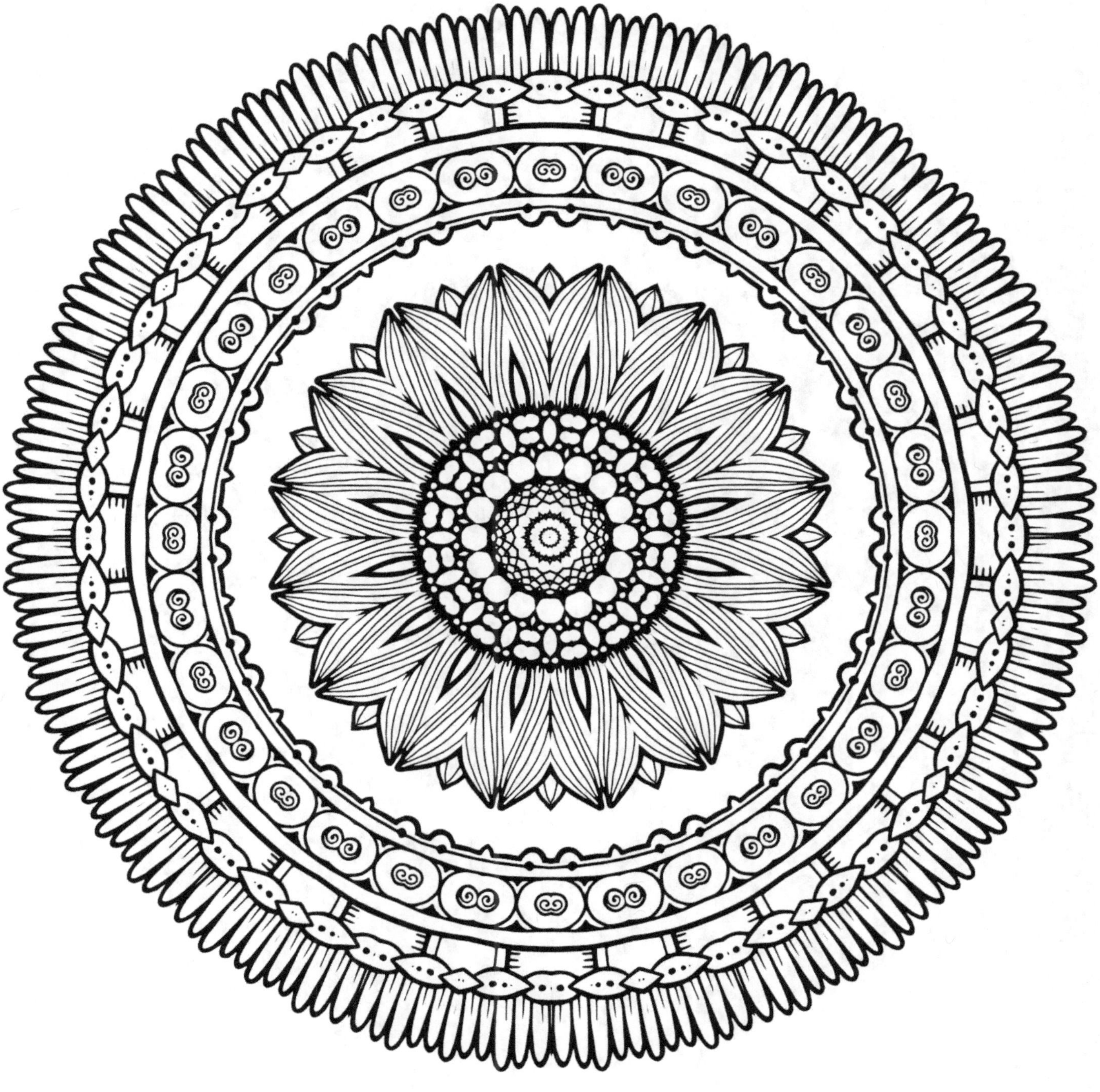

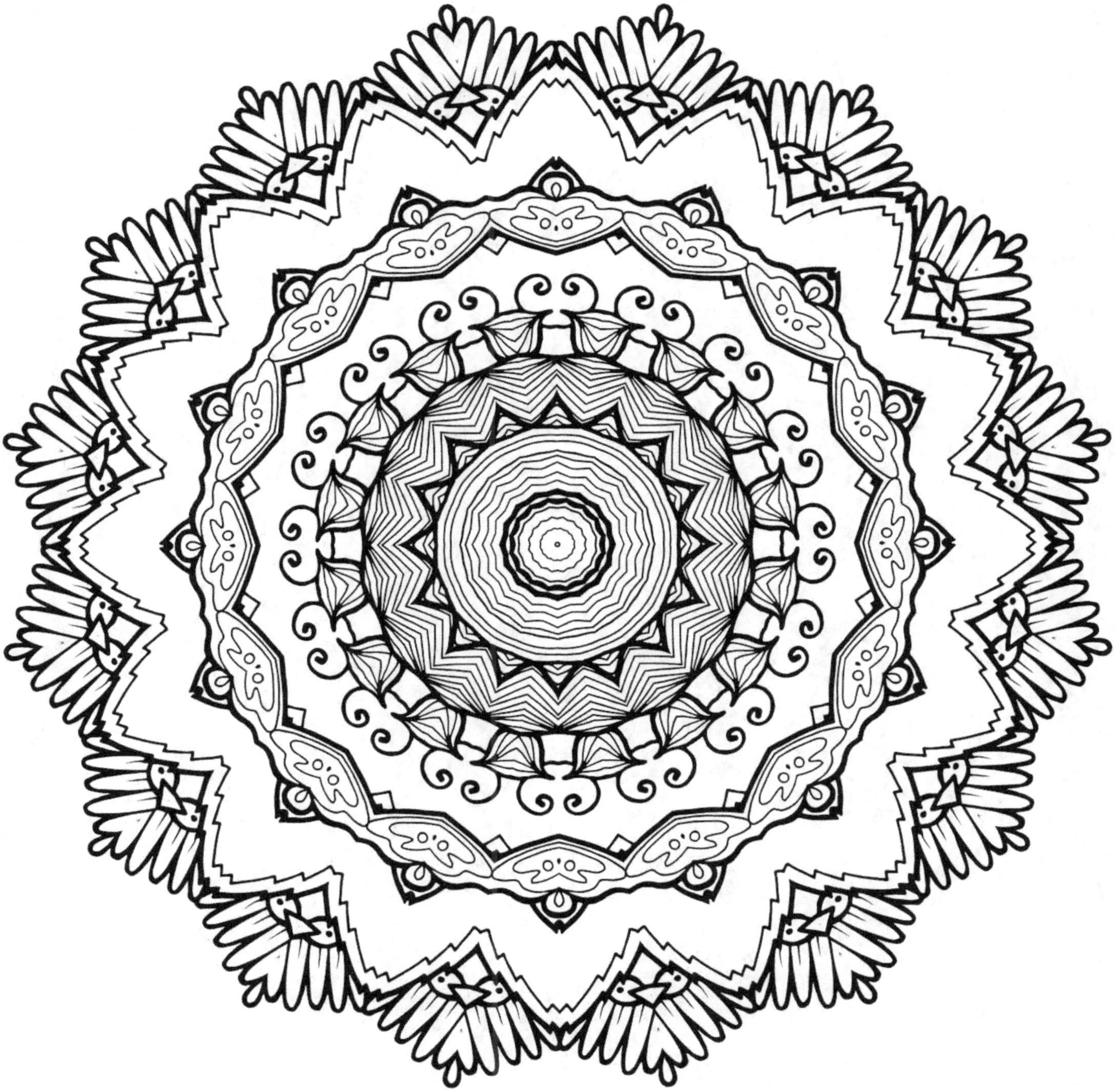

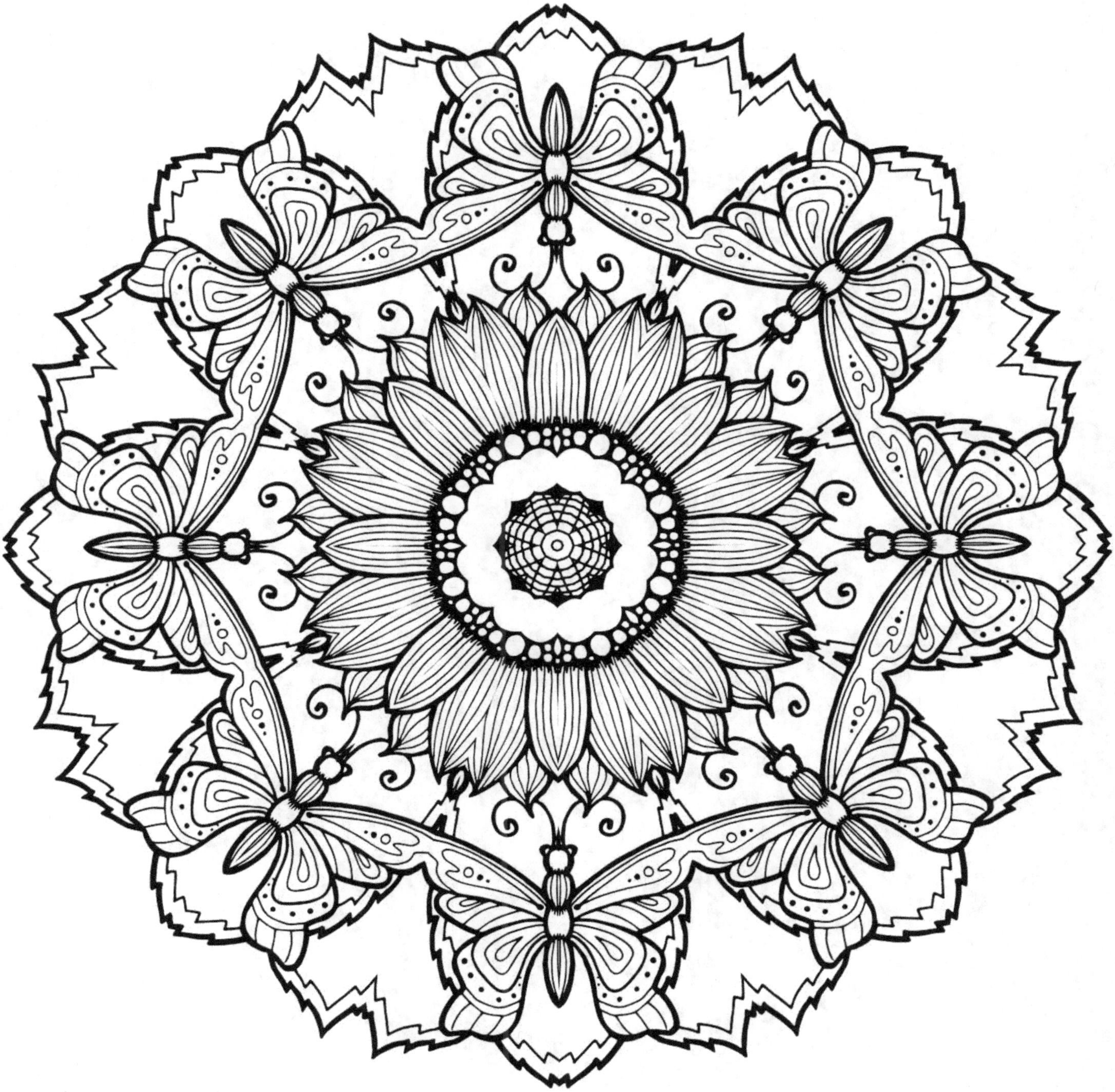

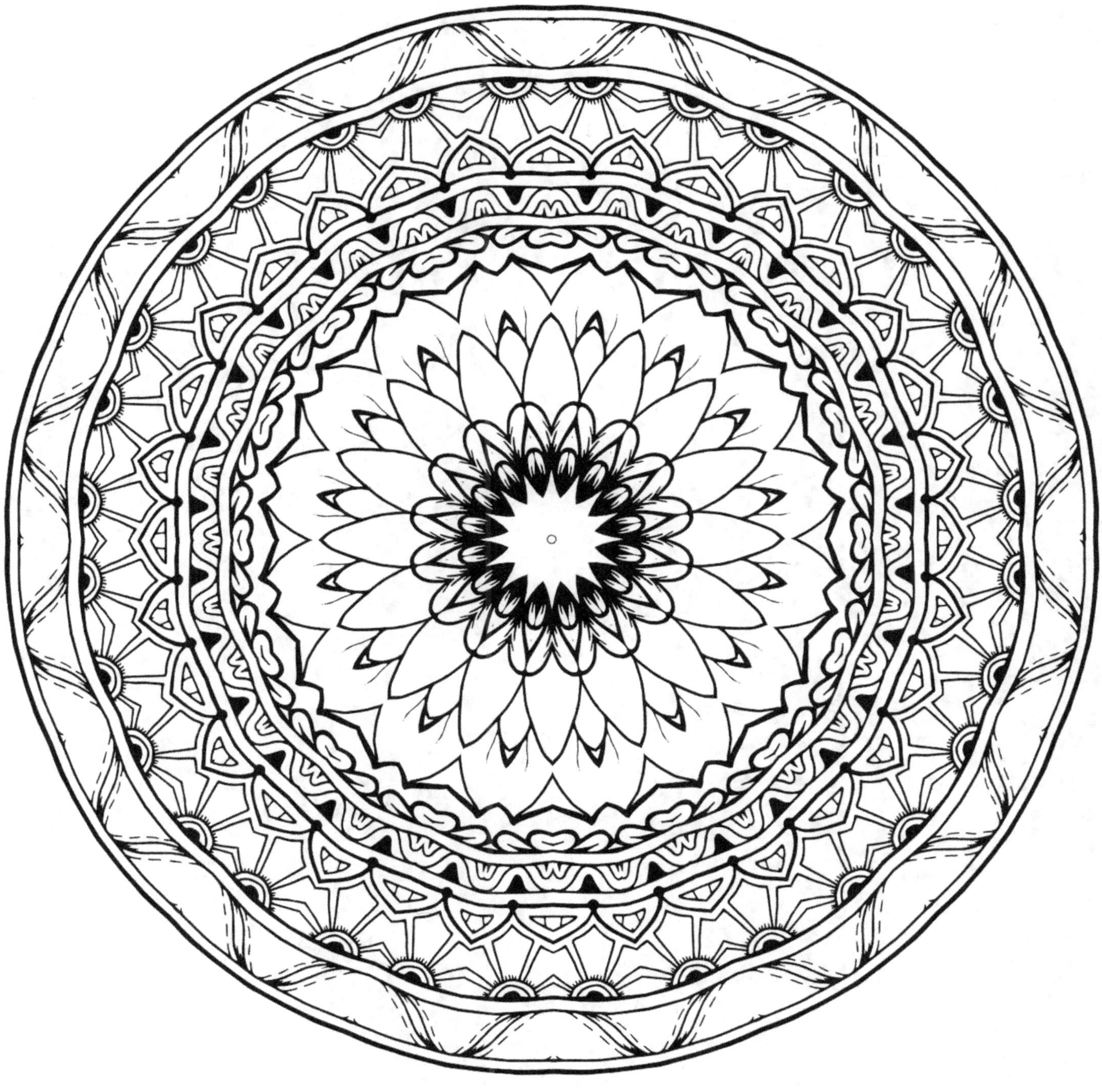

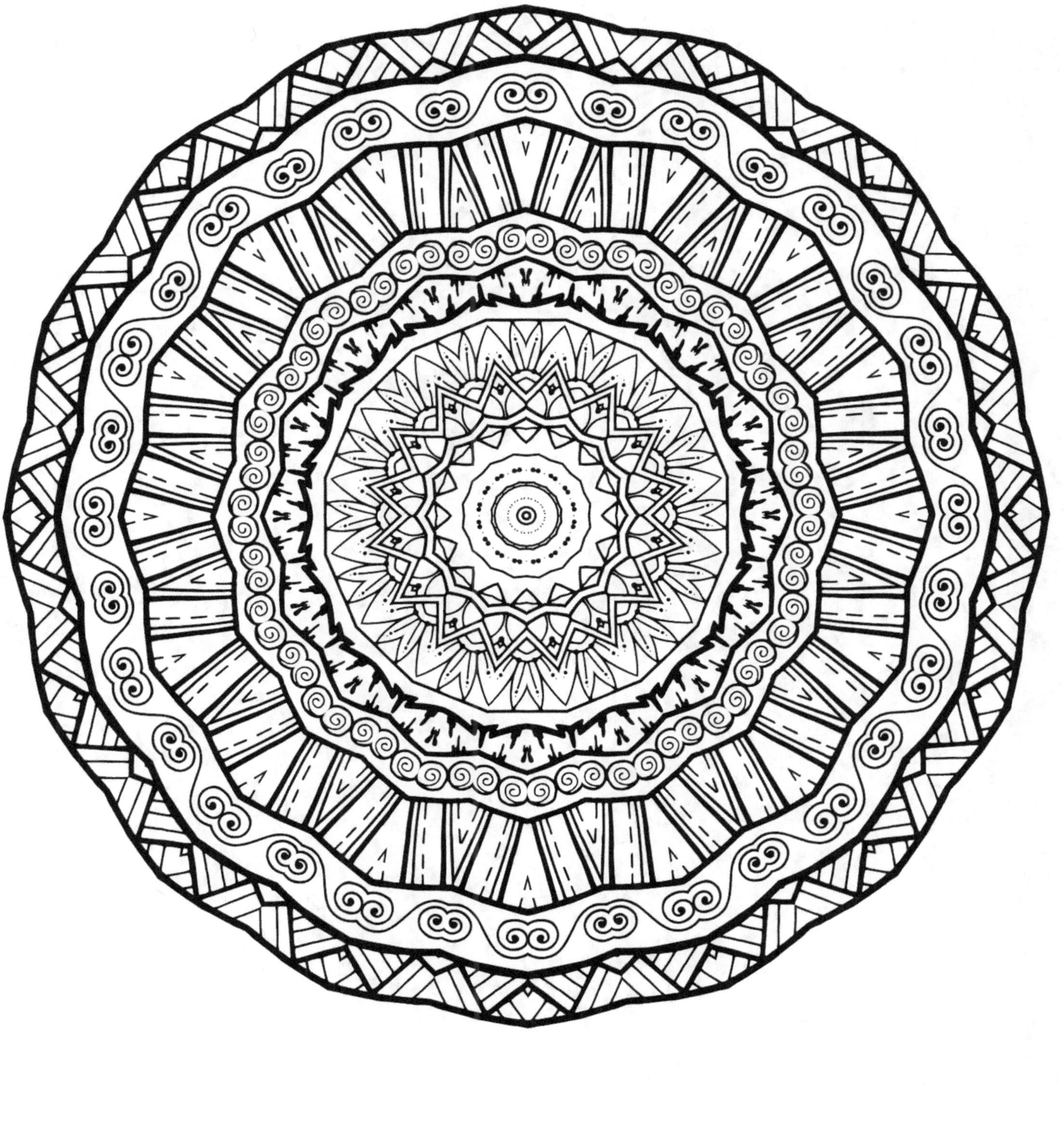

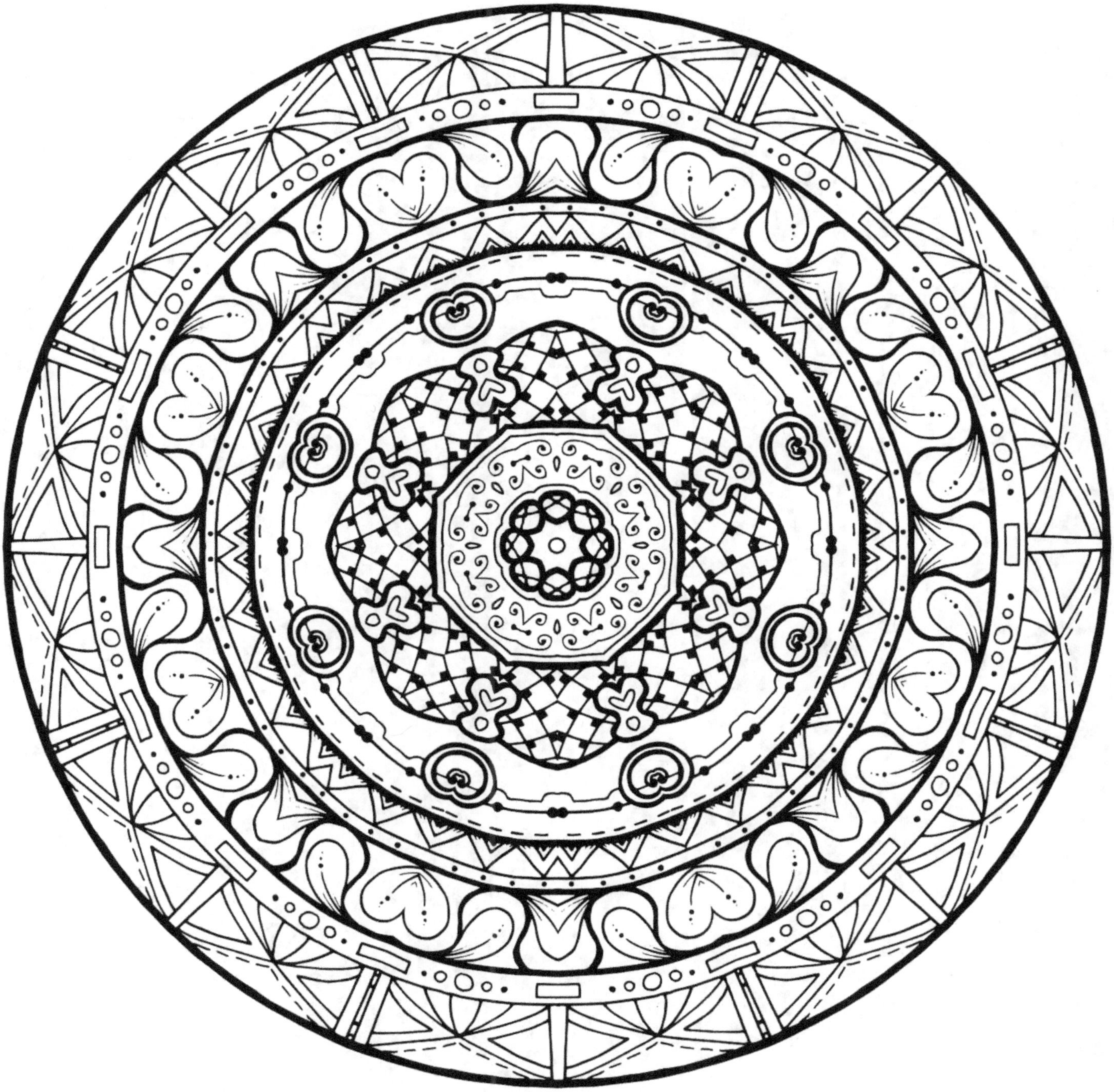

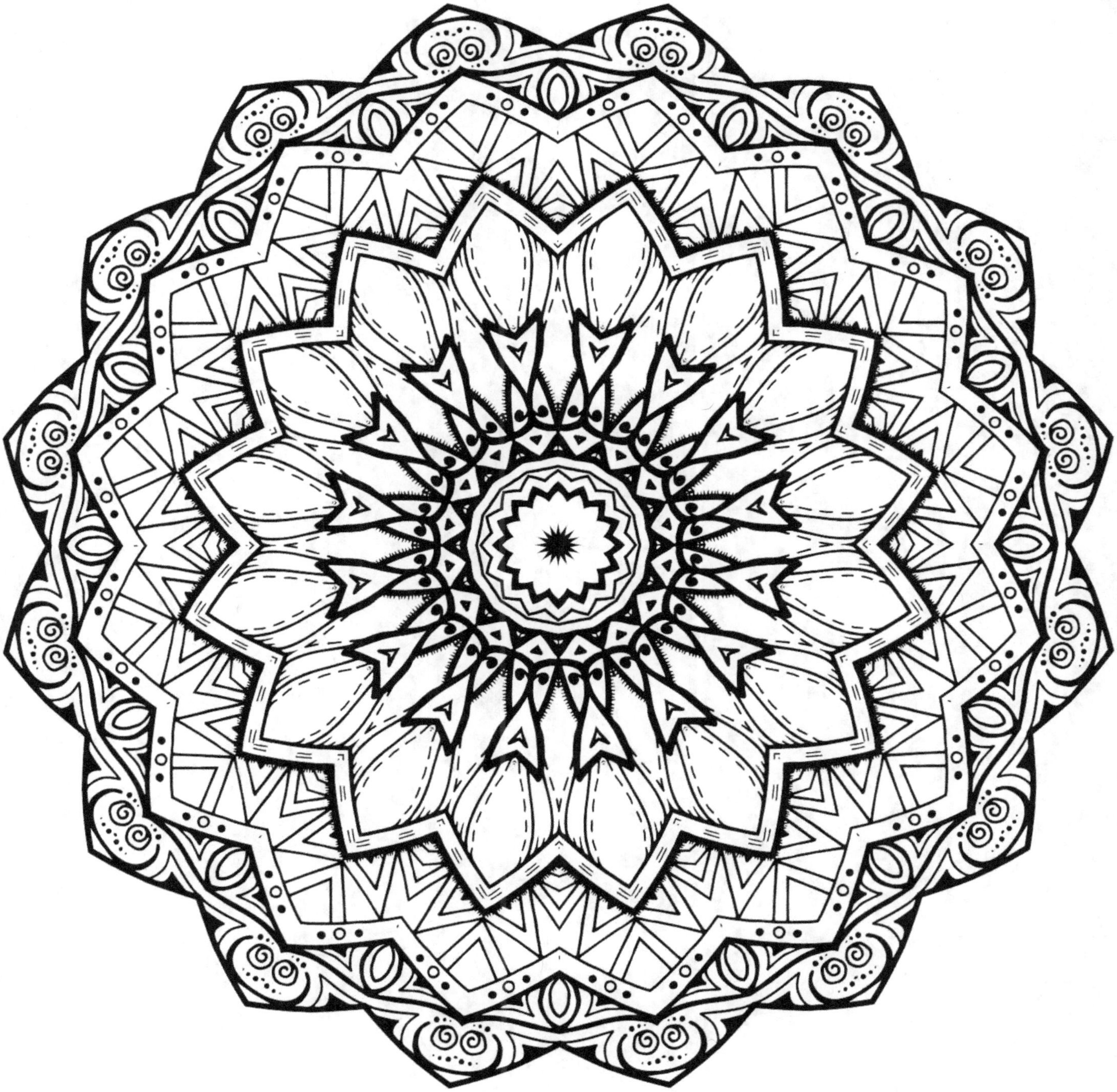

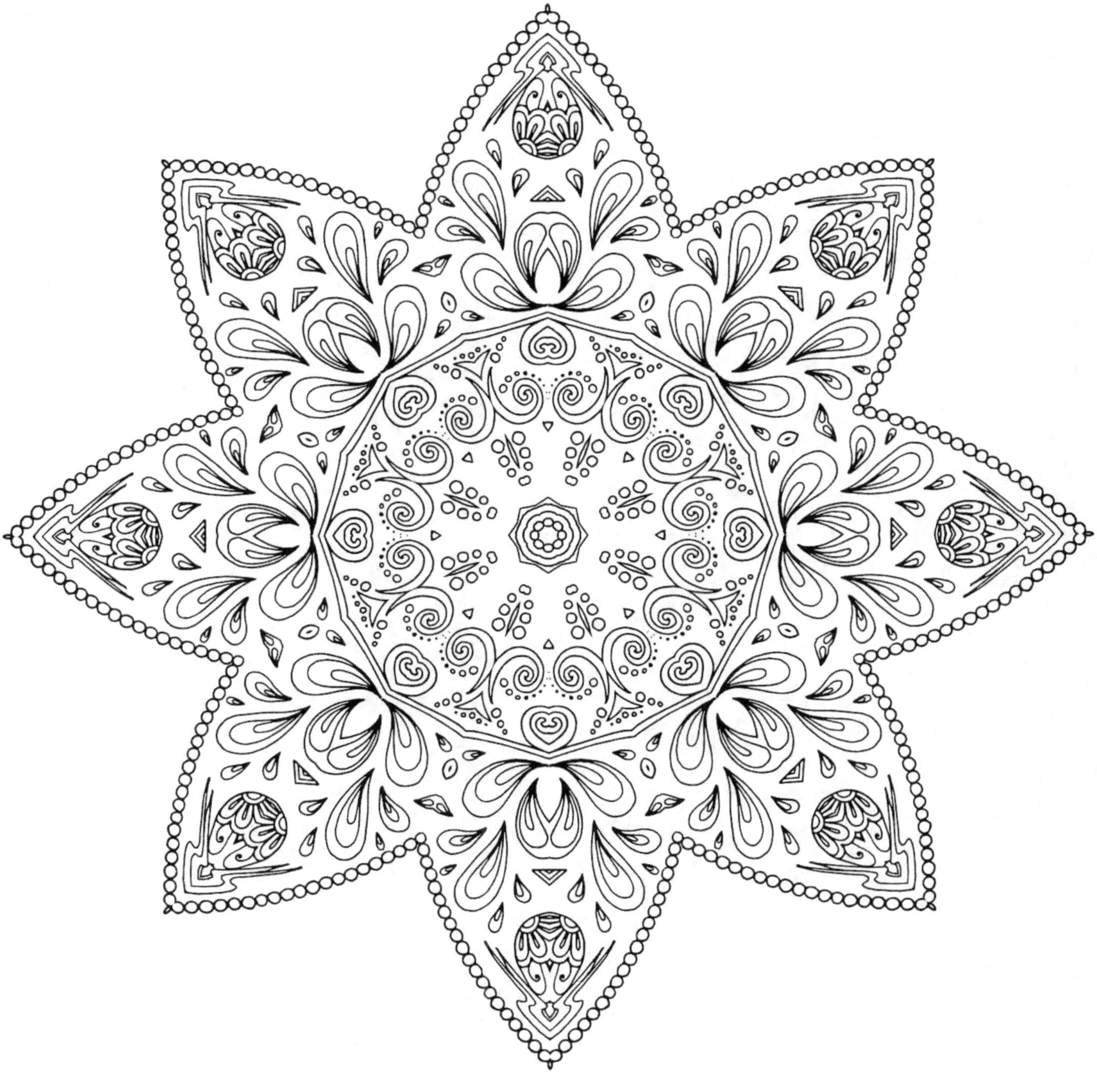

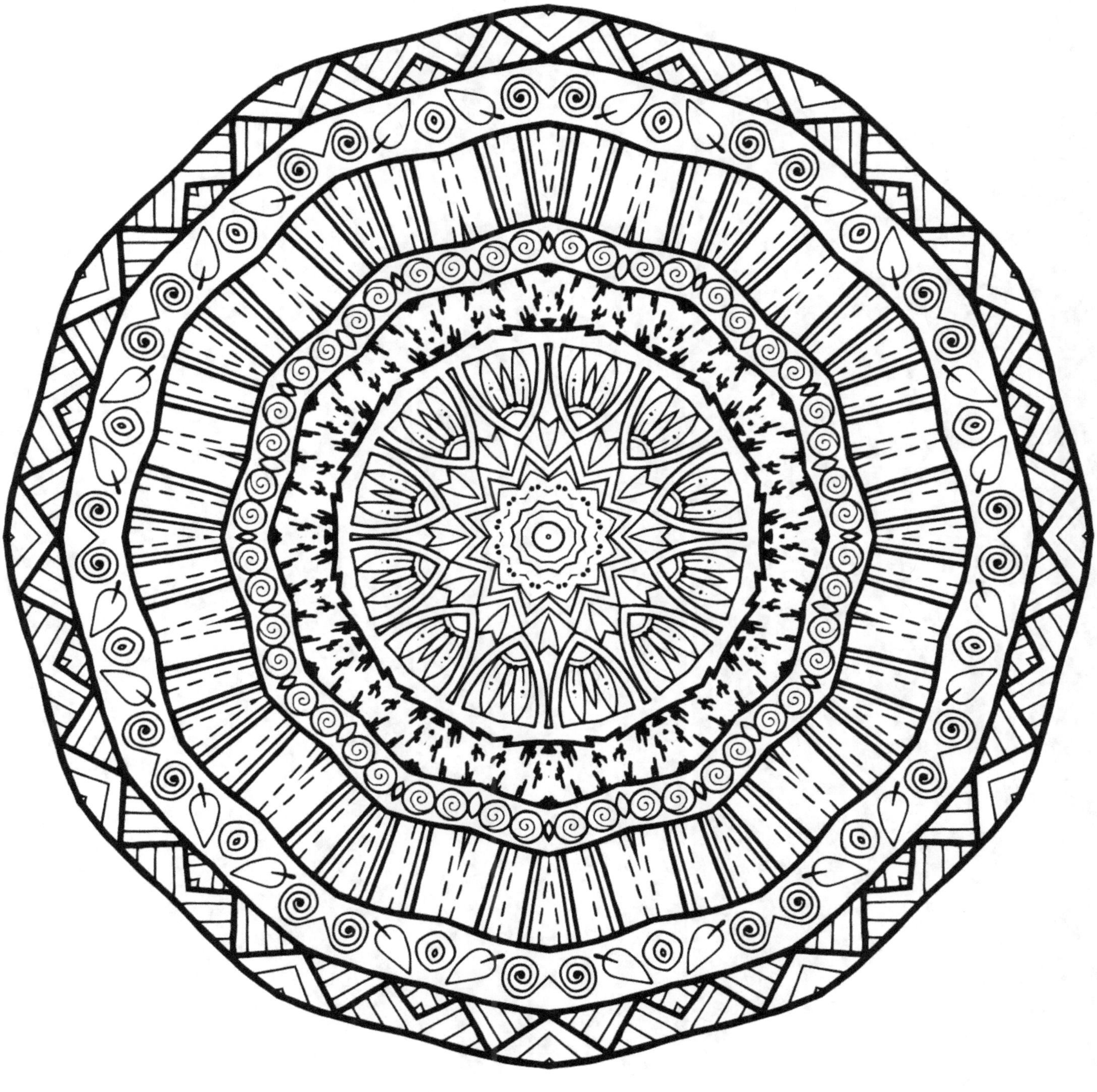

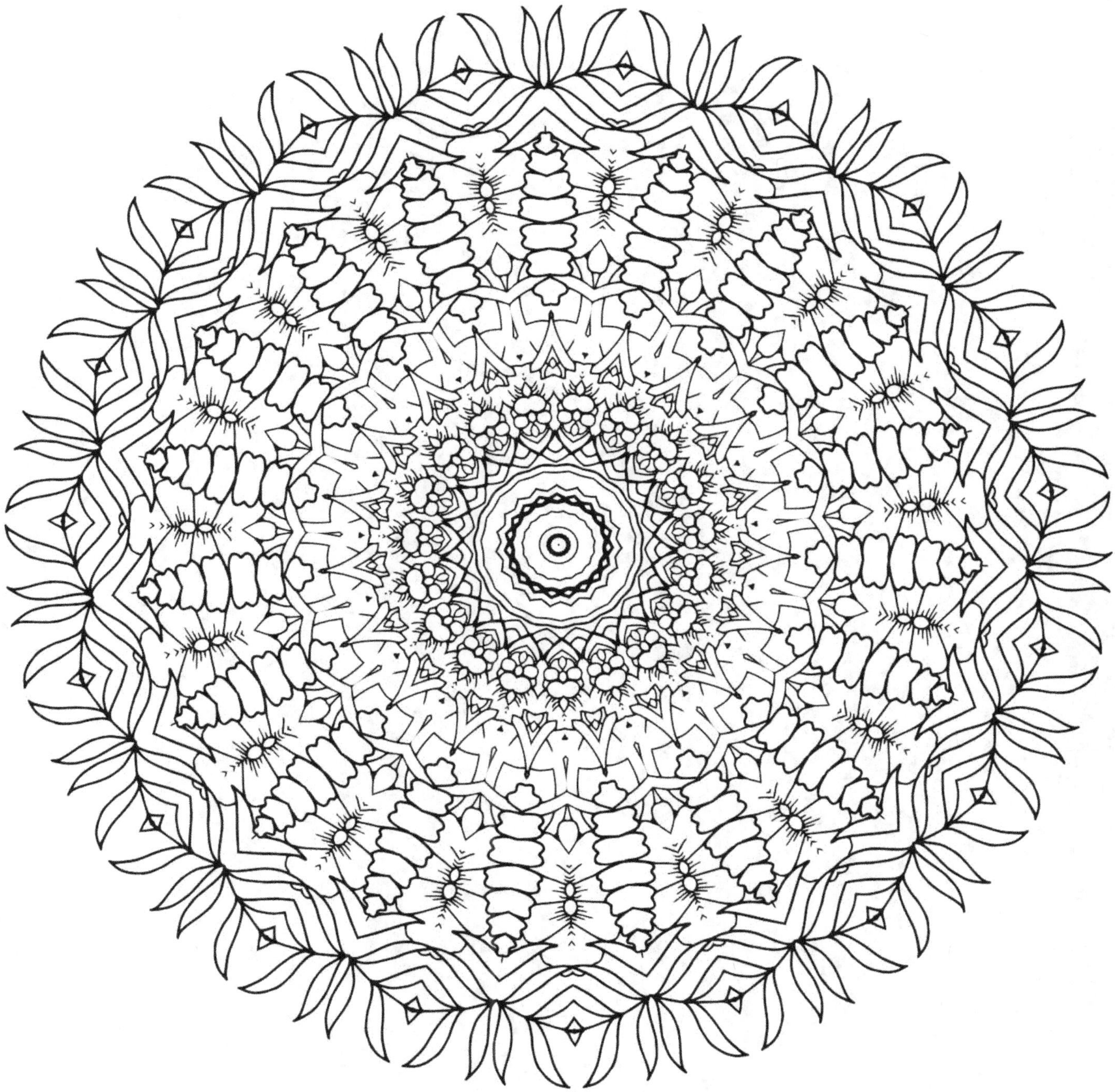

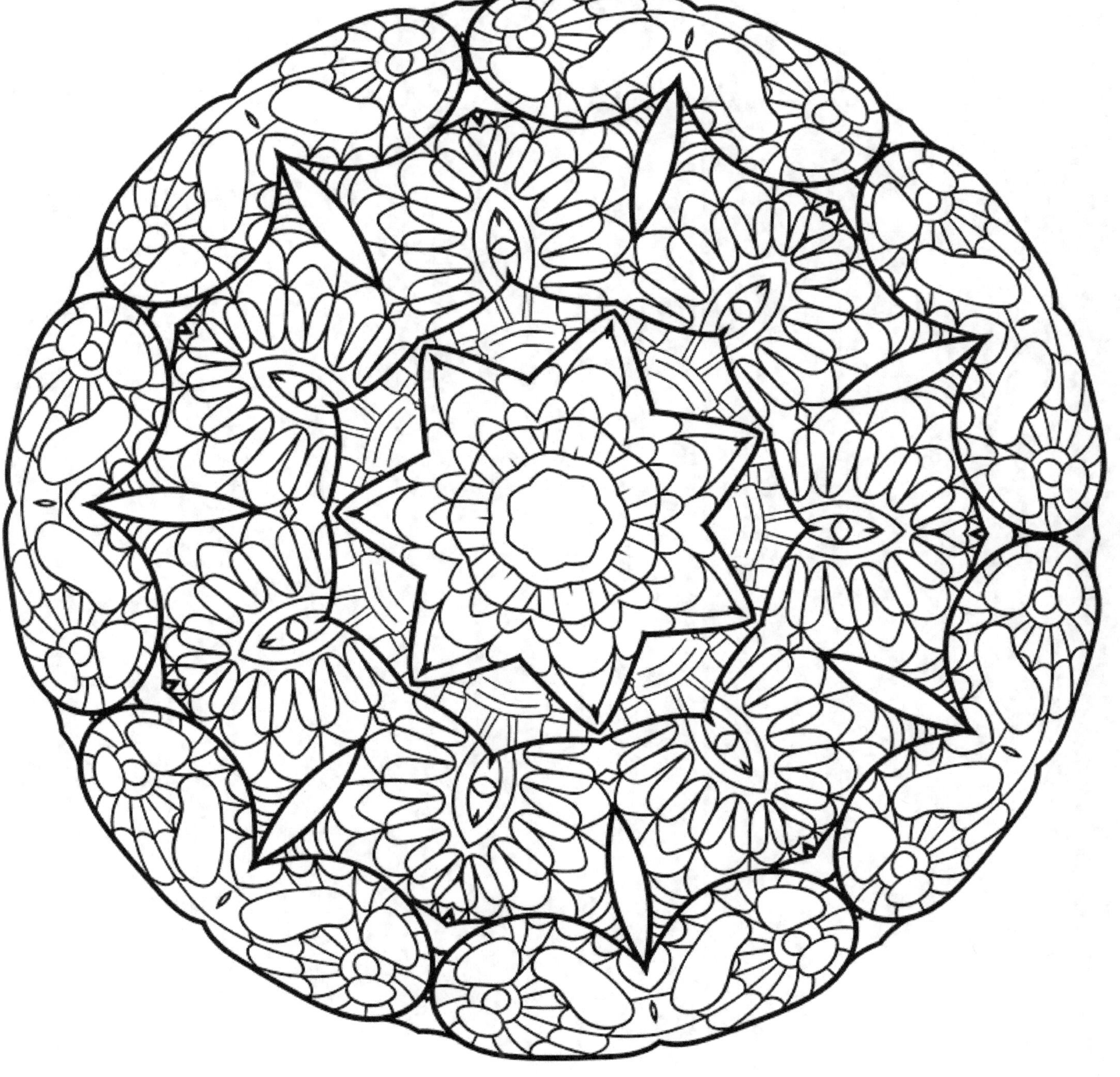

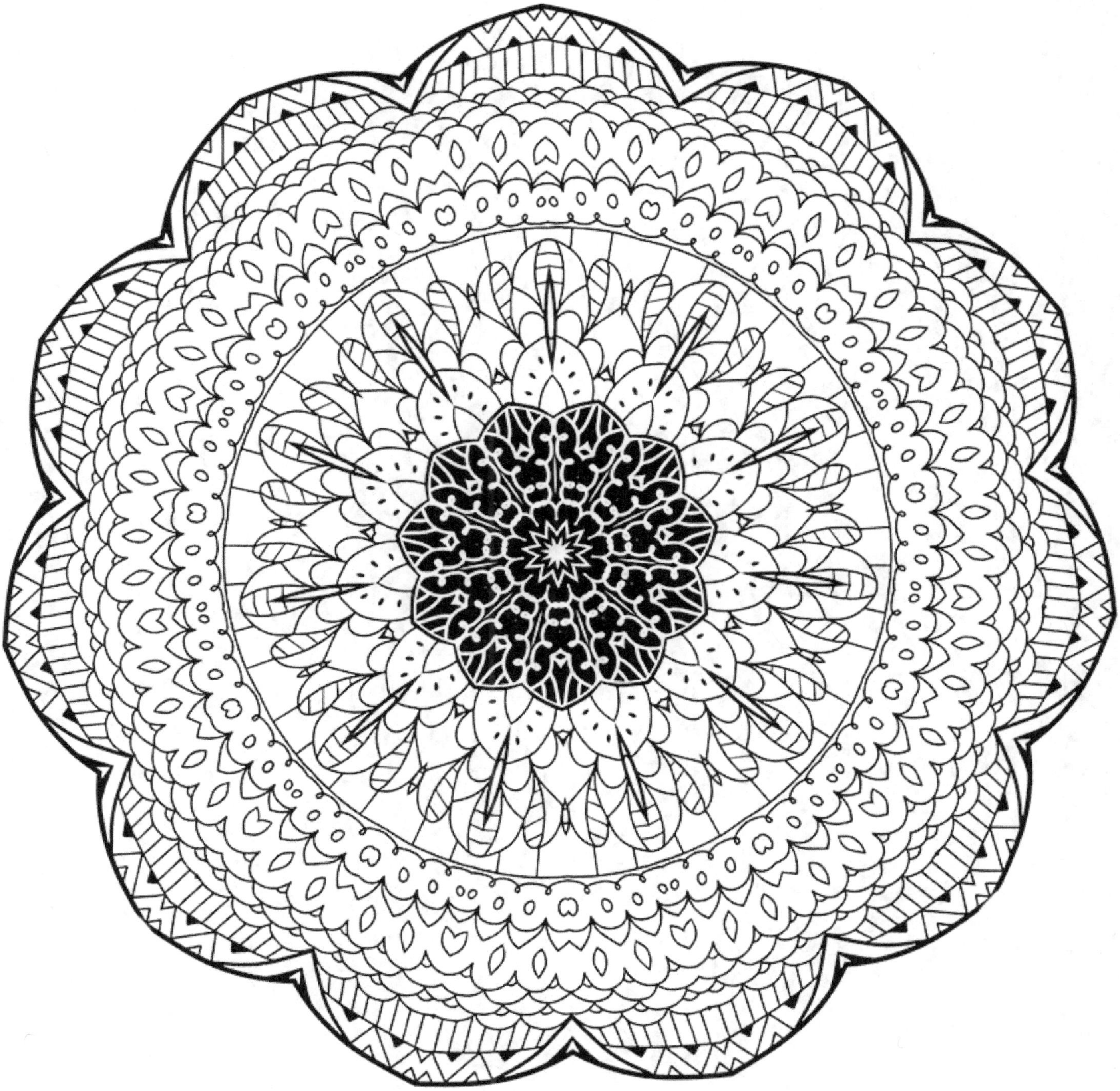

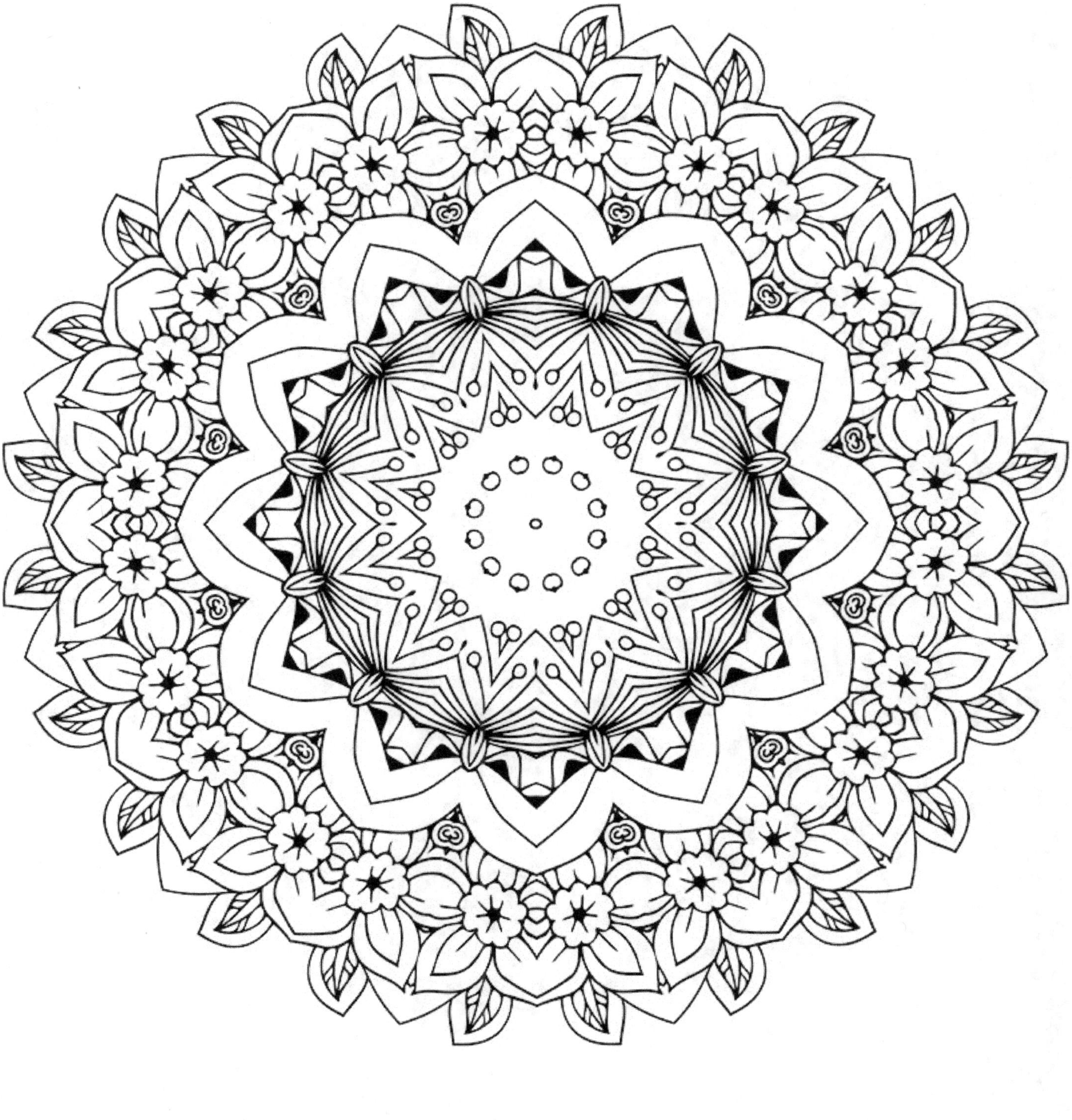

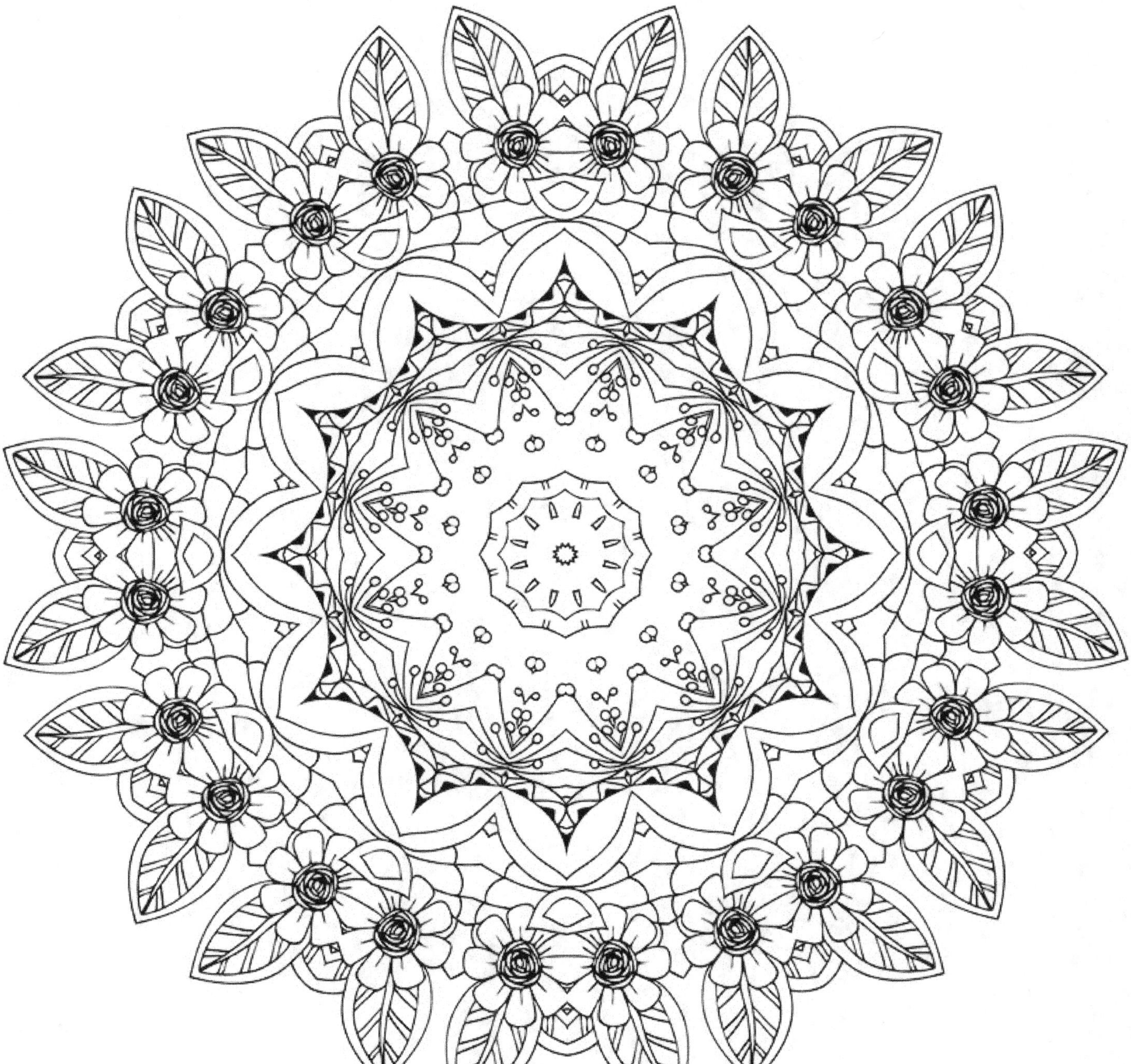

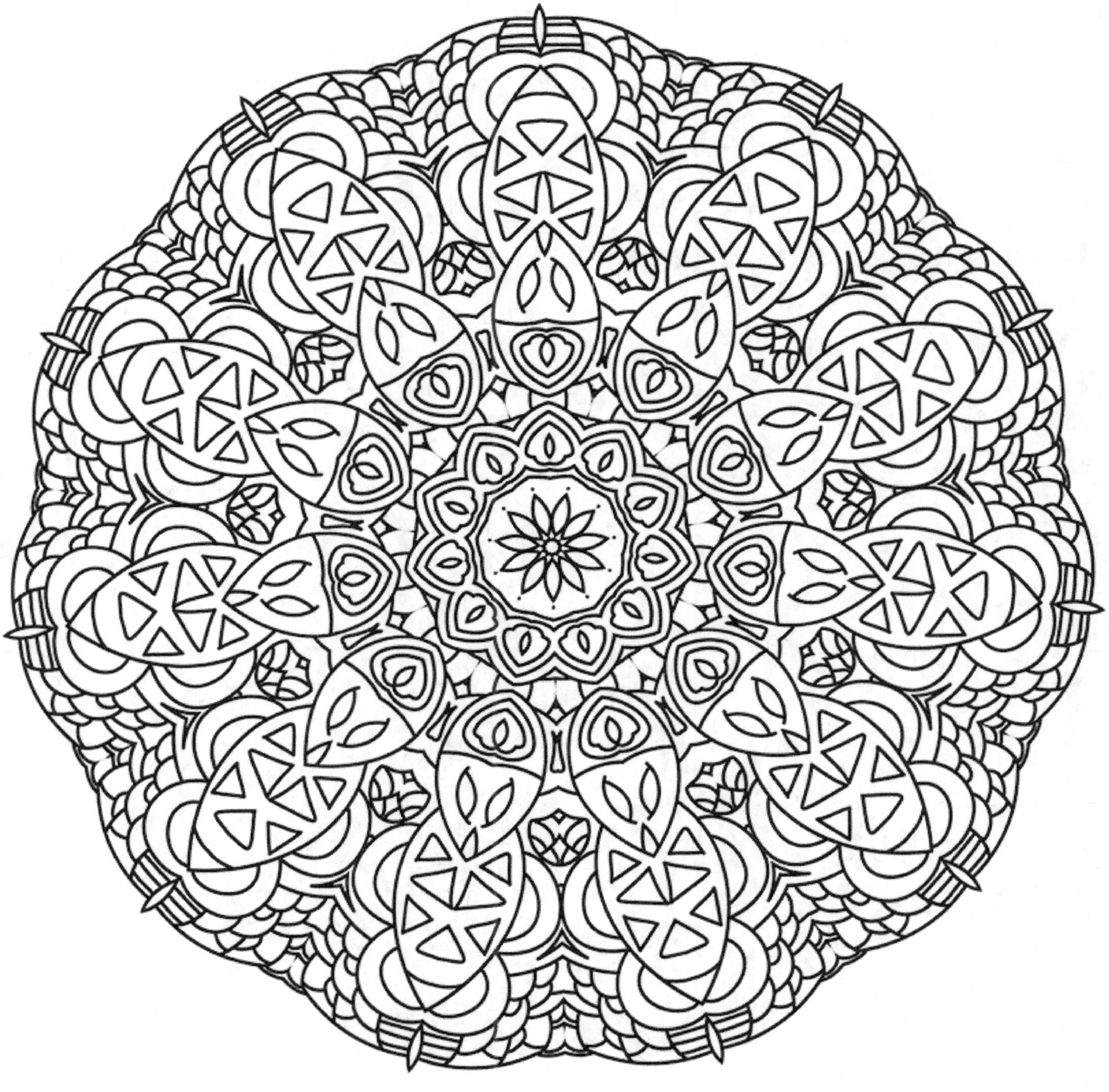

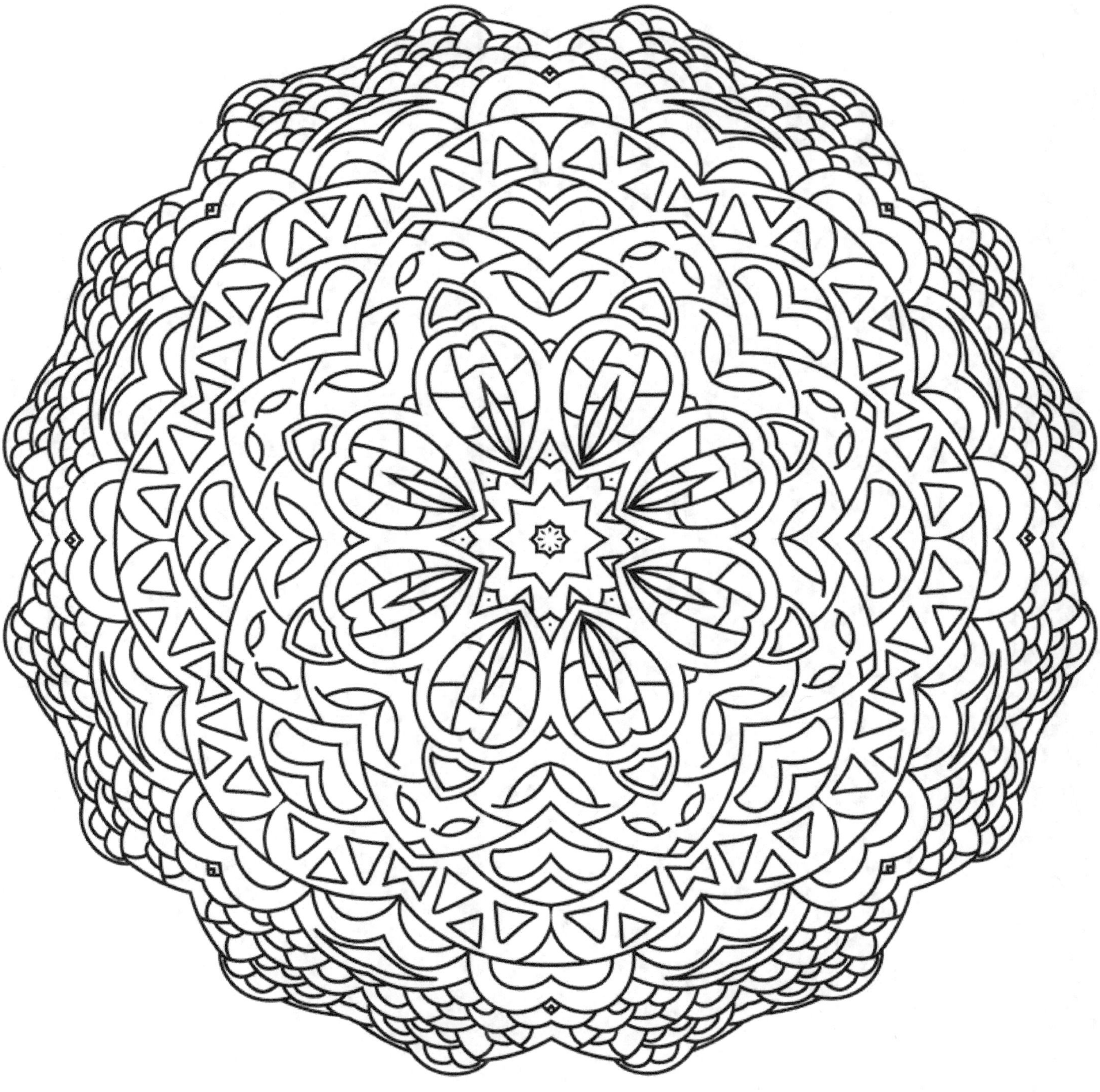

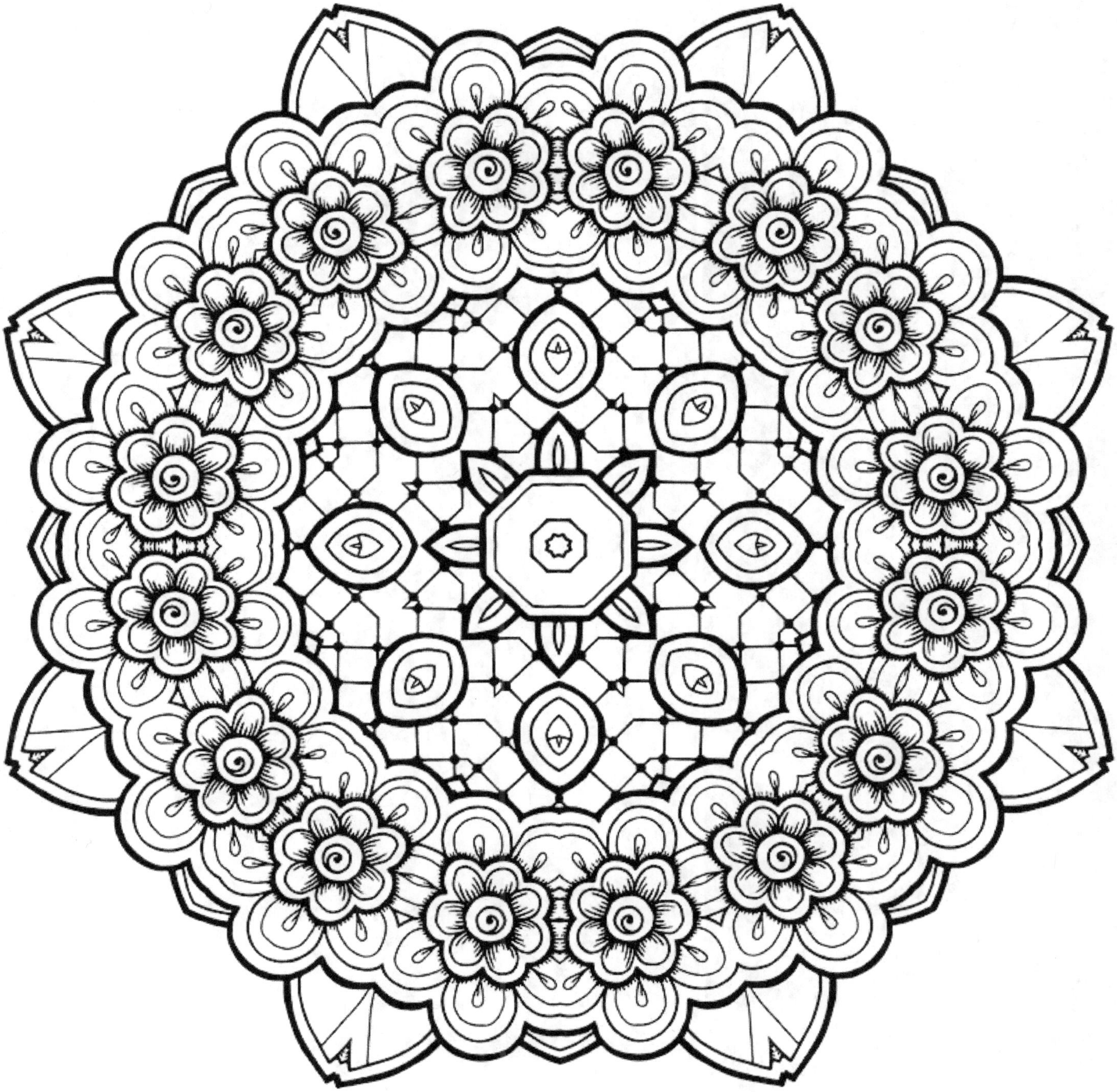

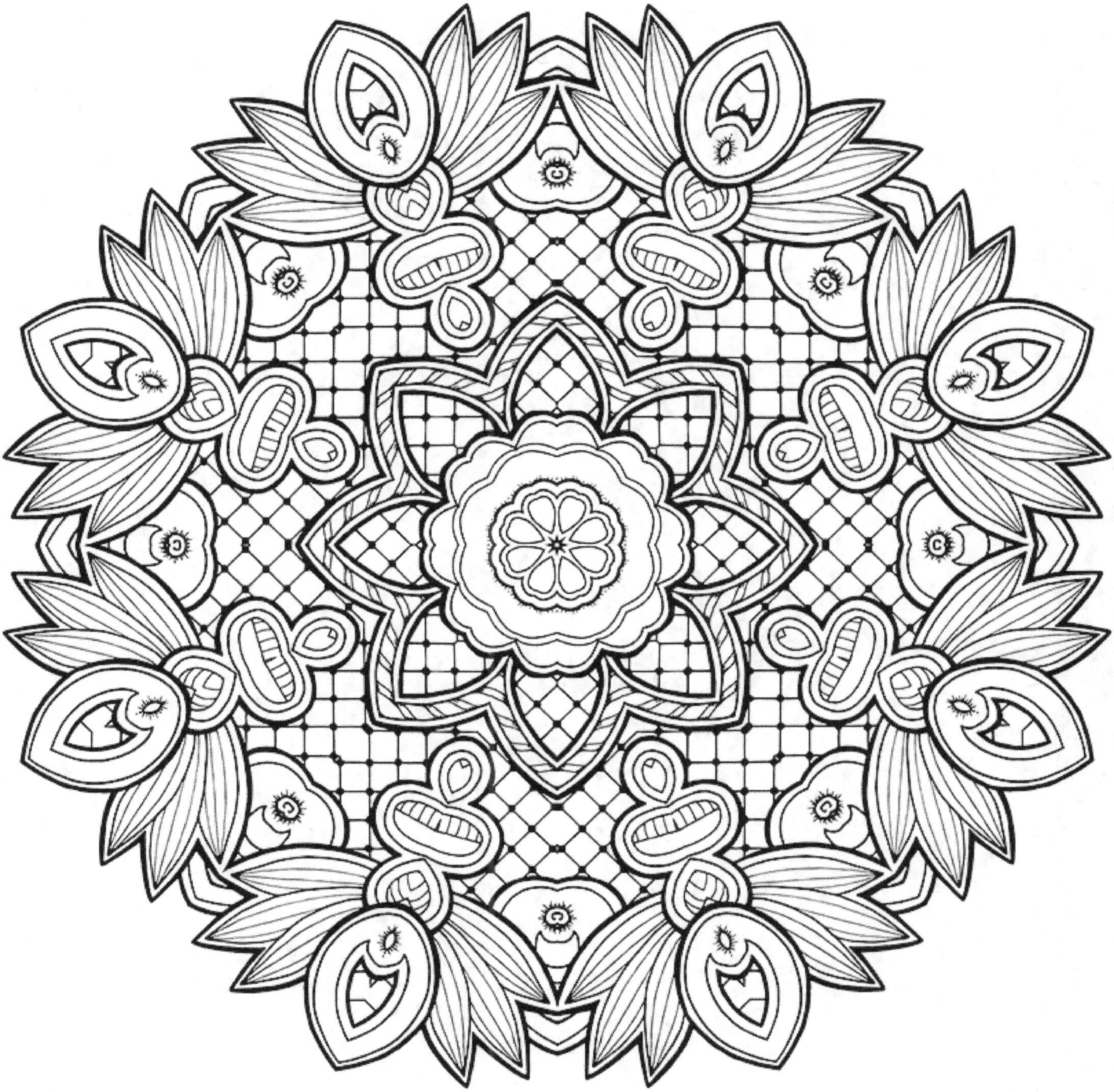

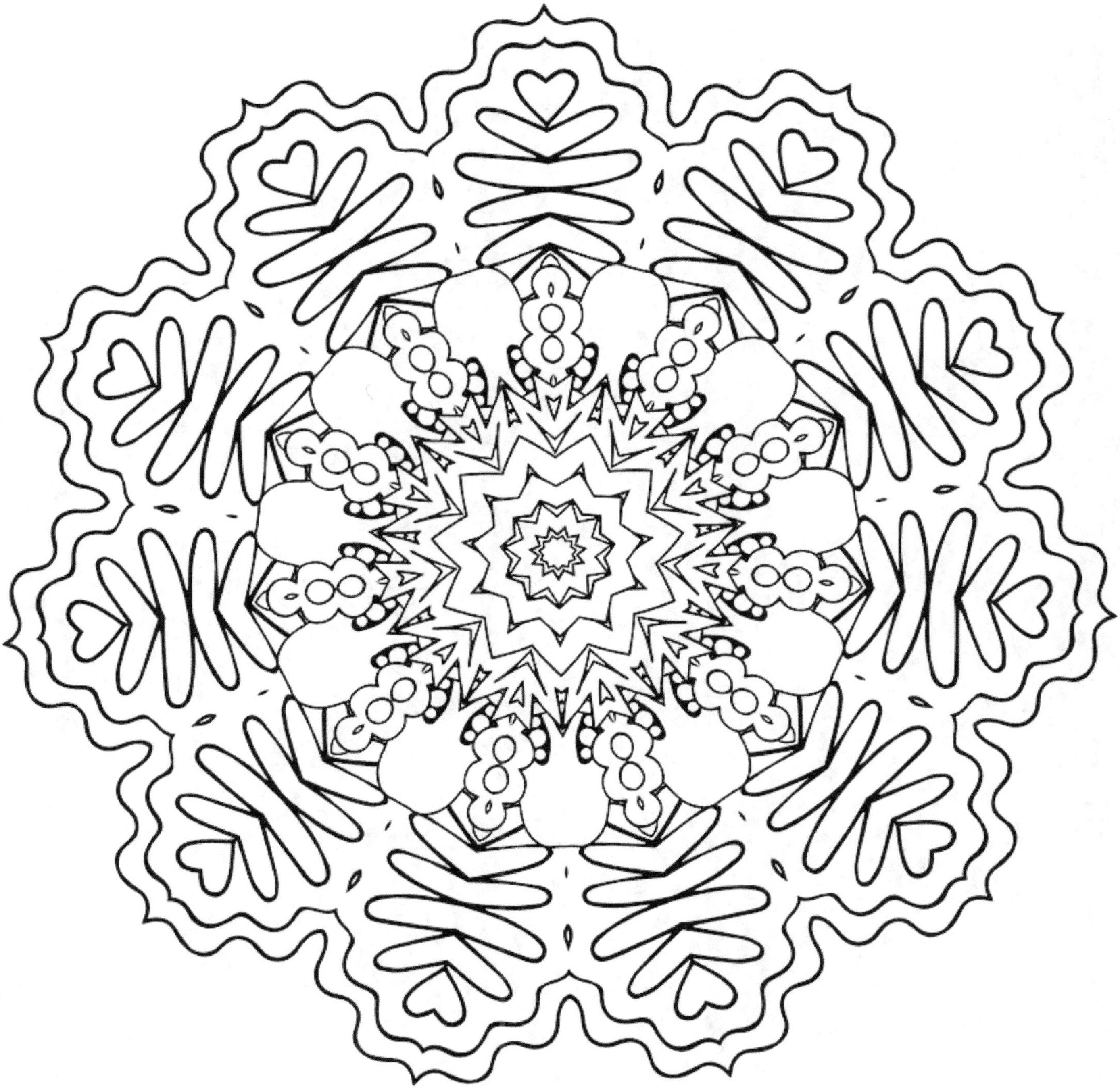

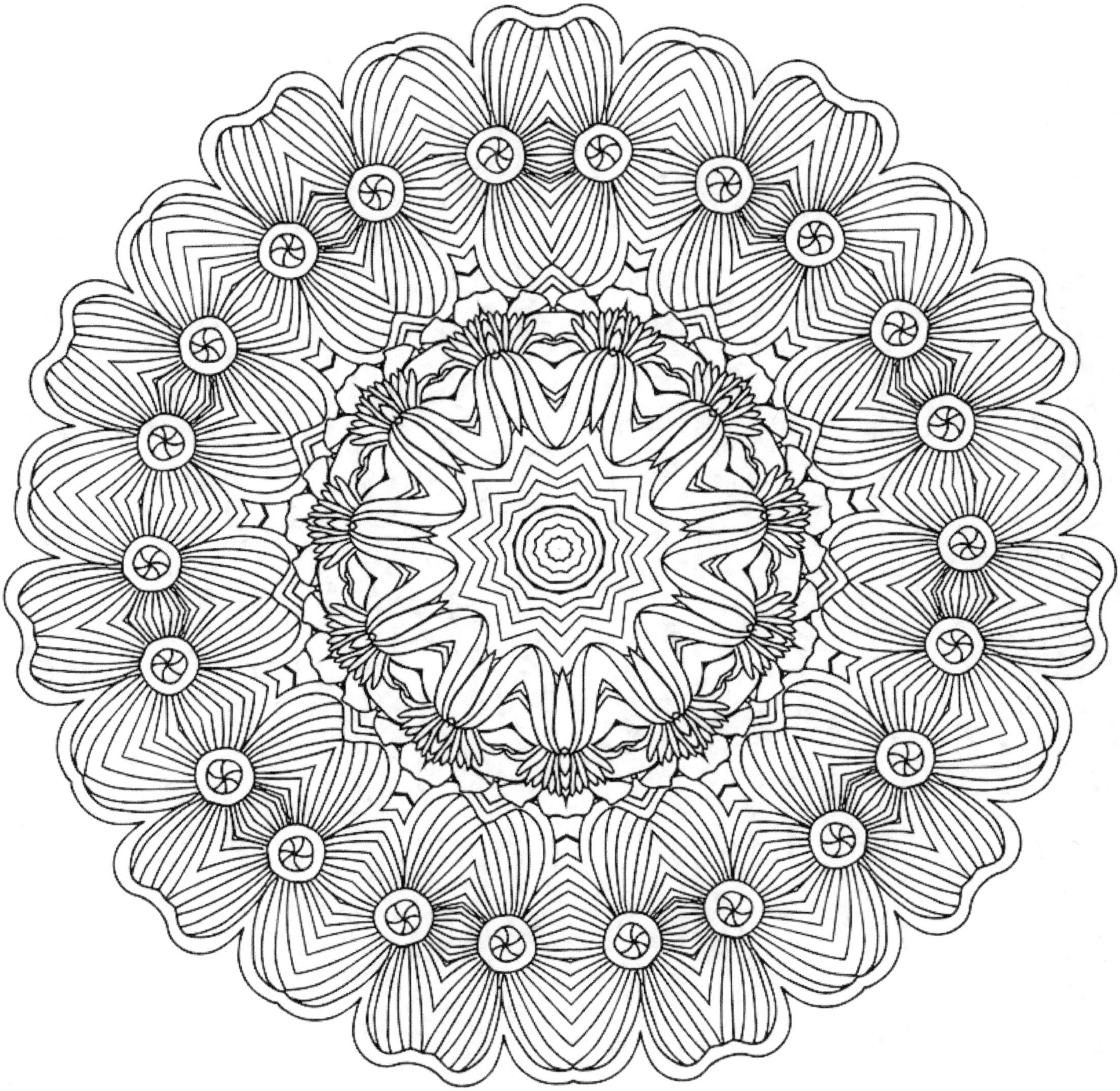

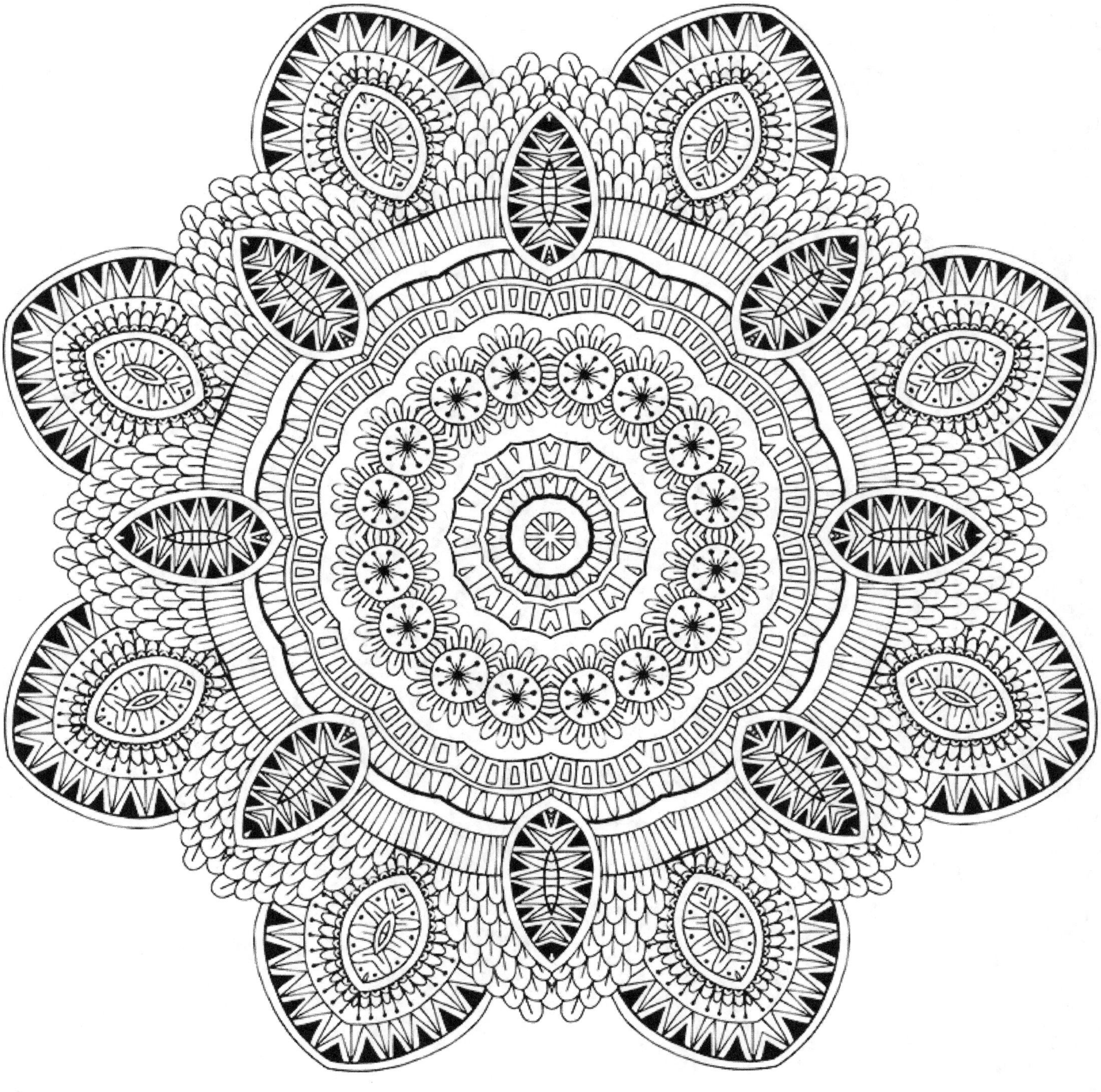

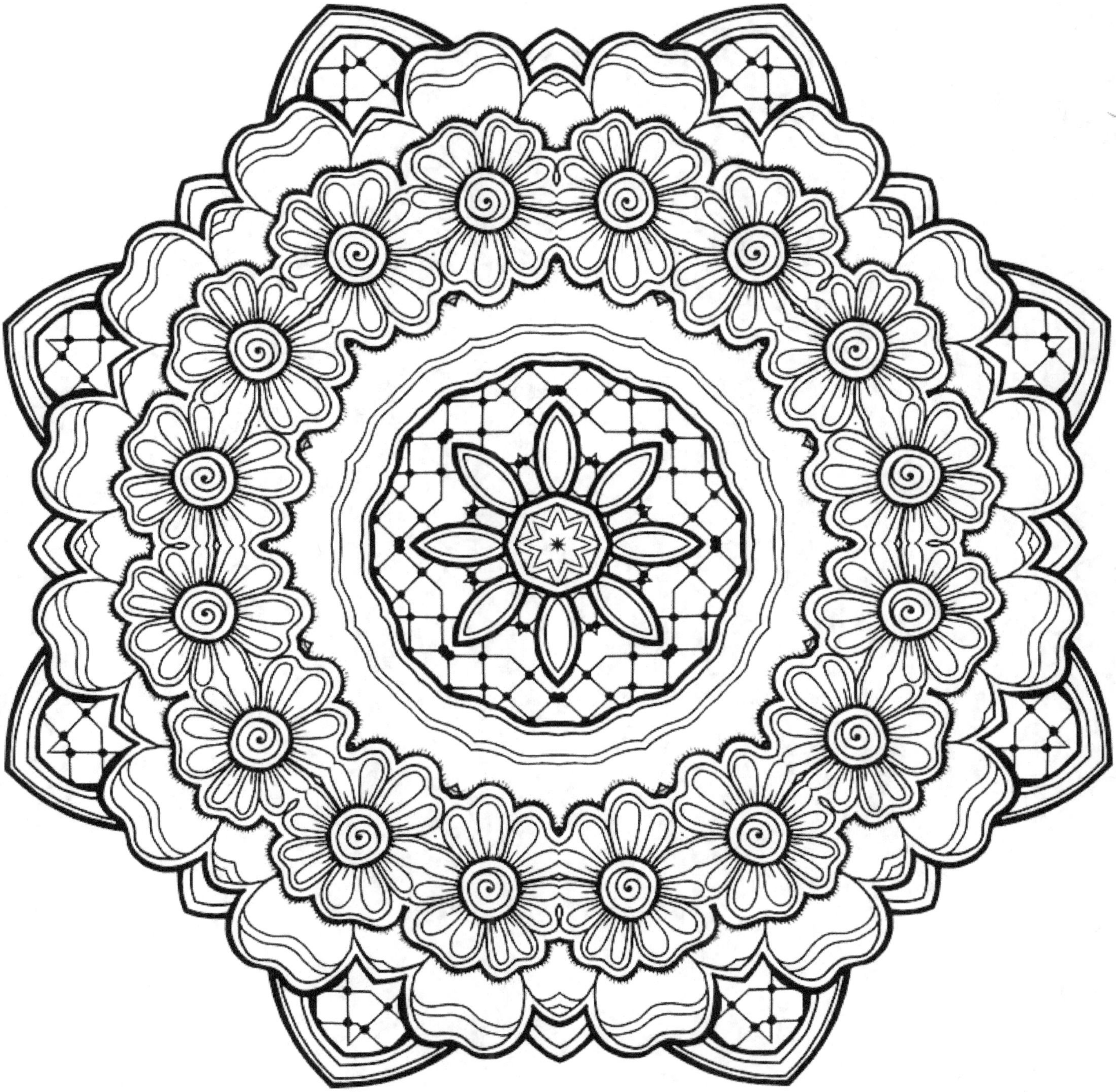

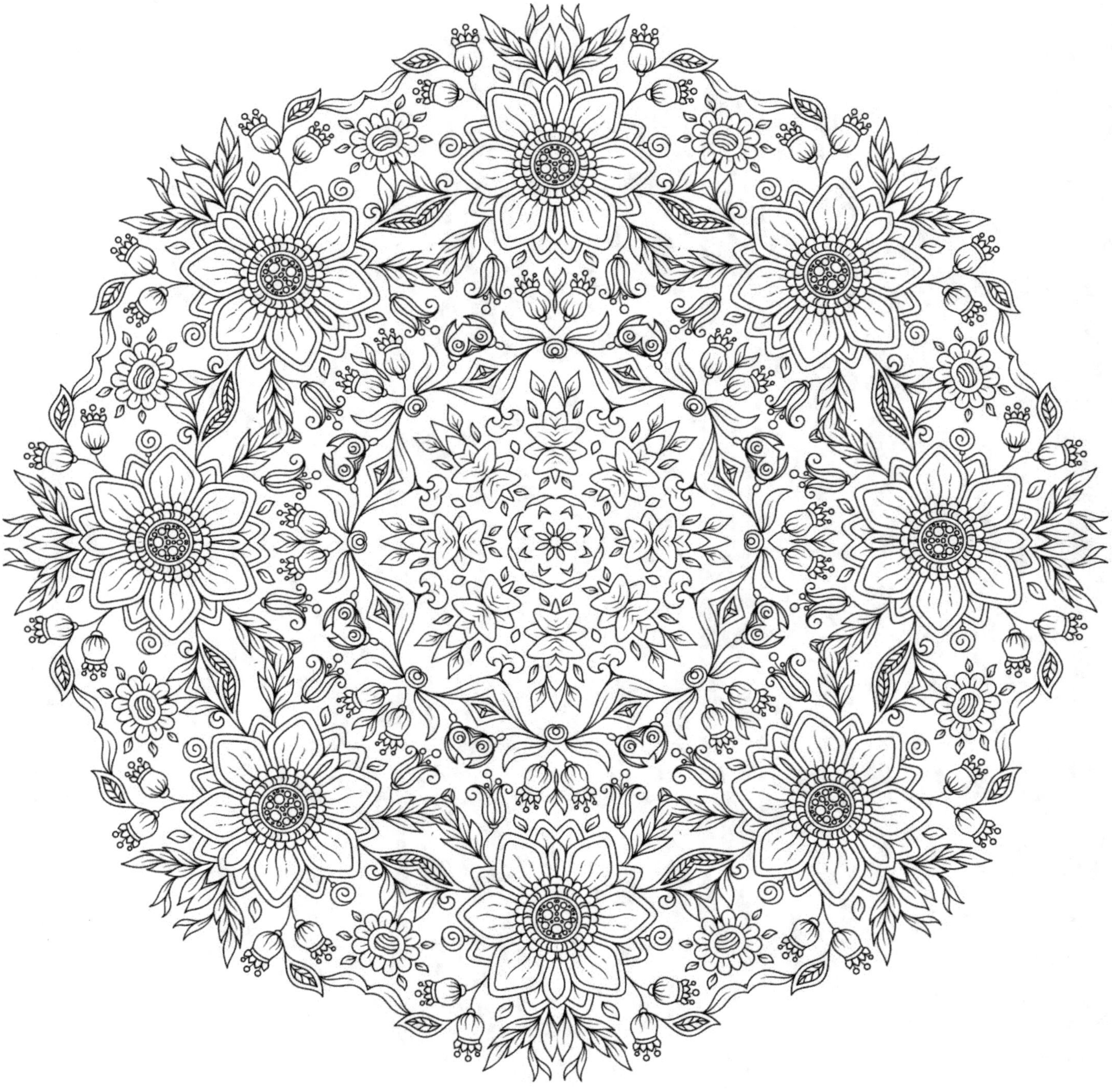

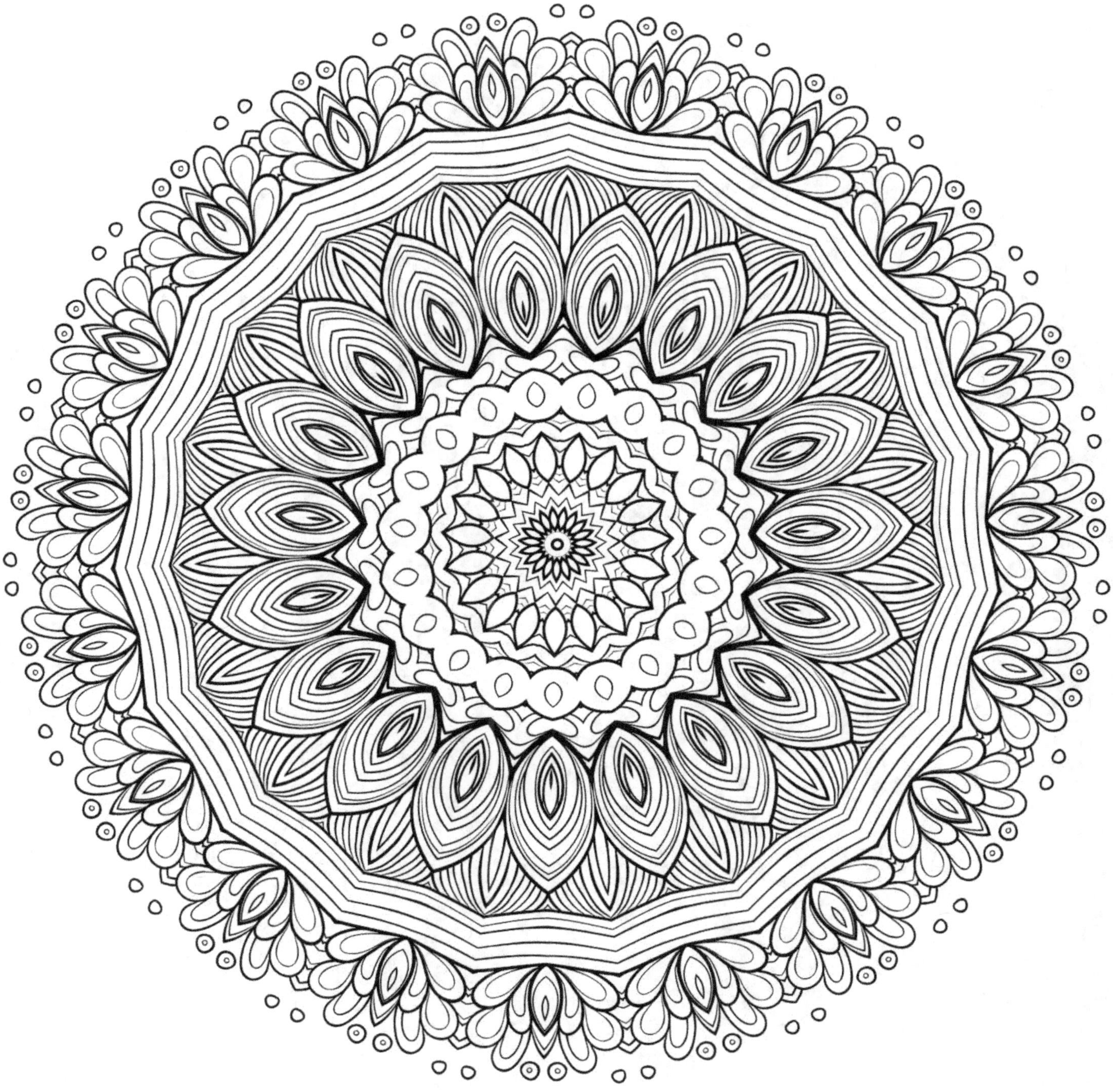

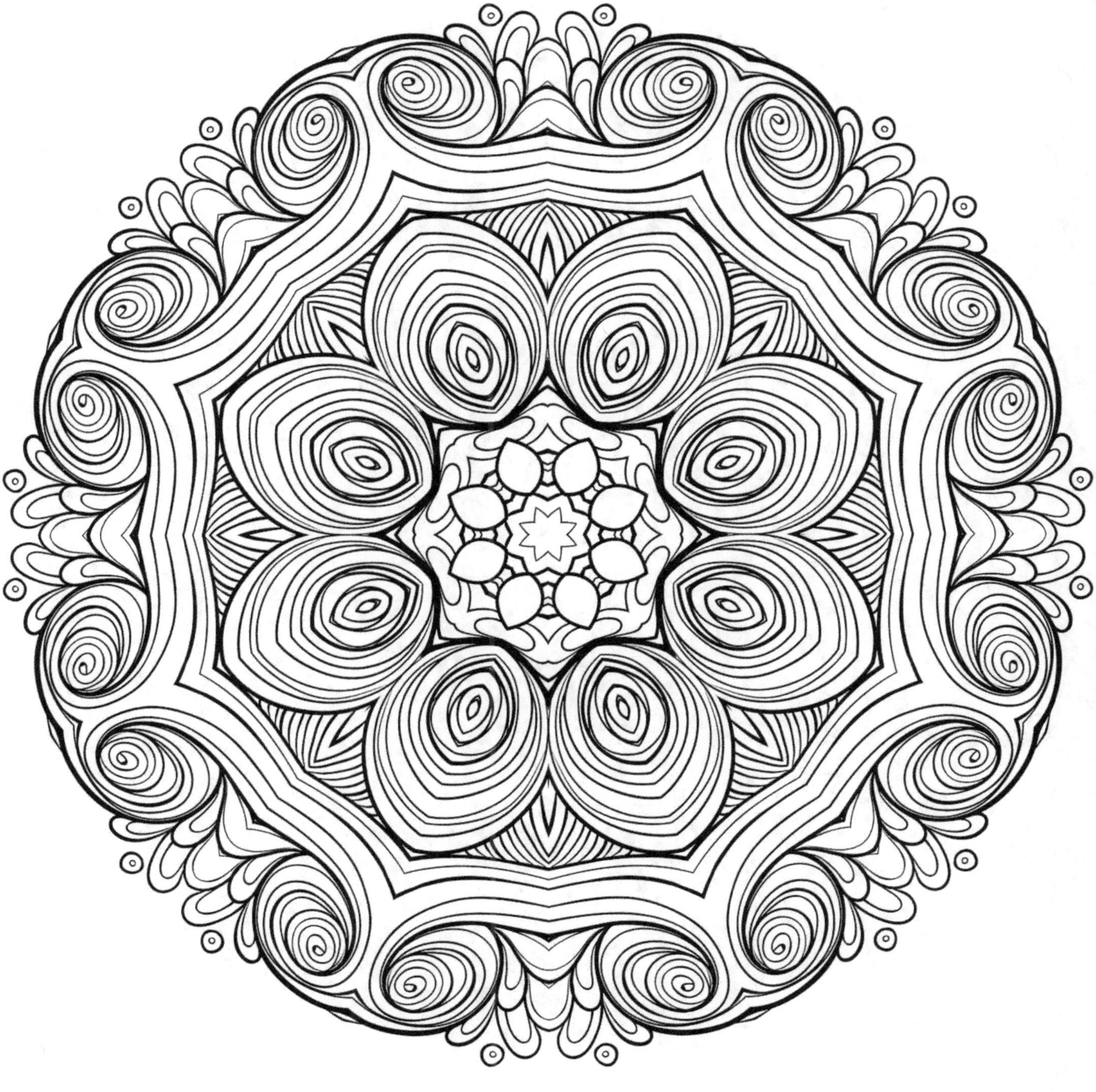

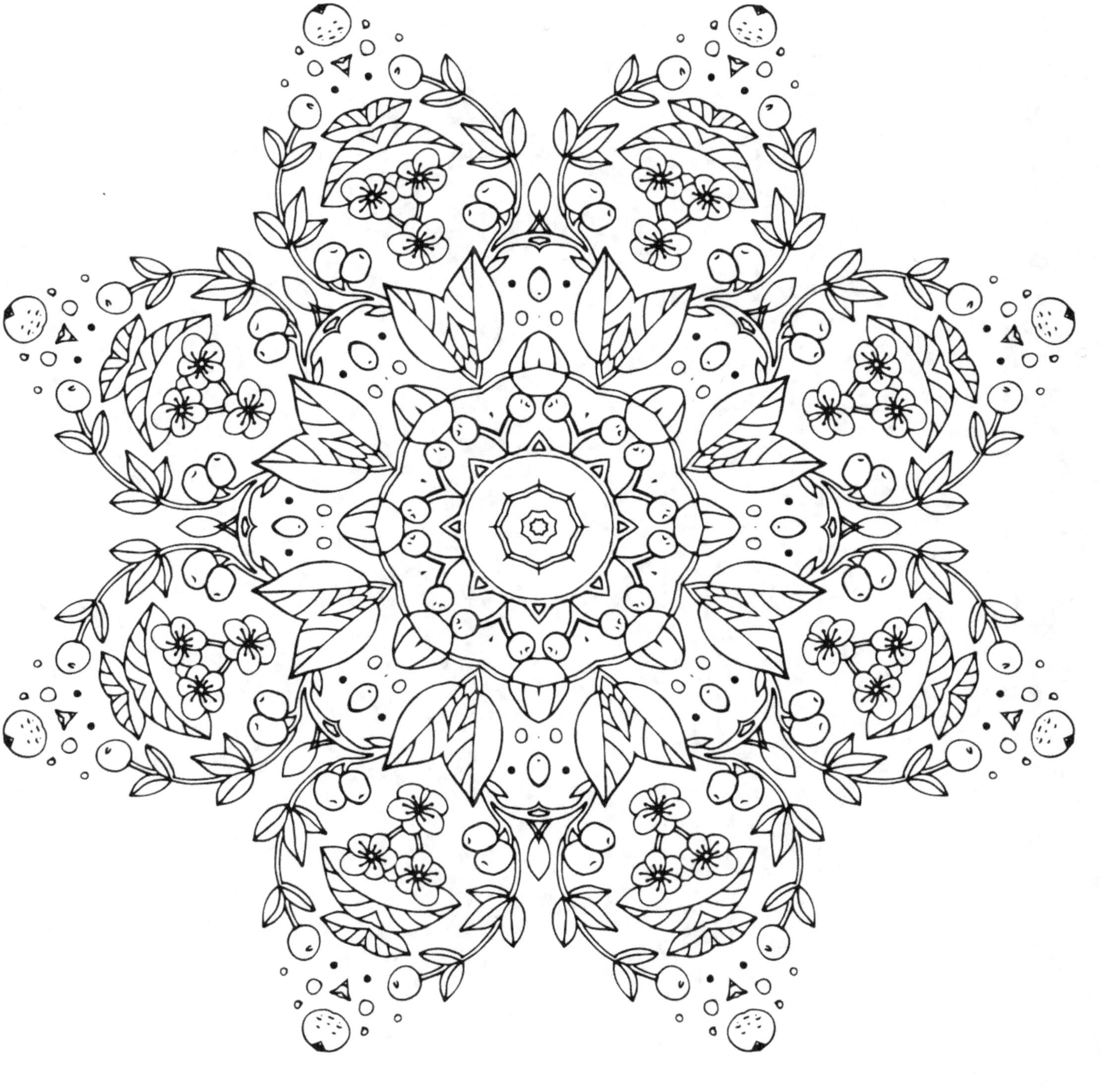

www.ingramcontent.com/pod-product-compliance
Lightning Source LLC
Chambersburg PA
CBHW081414280526
45788CB00009B/3094
* 9 7 8 1 5 4 4 7 4 2 8 7 8 *